Birds of the Eastern Forest: 2

PAINTINGS BY
J. FENWICK LANSDOWNE

TEXT BY
JOHN A. LIVINGSTON

Birds of the Eastern Forest : 2

HOUGHTON MIFFLIN COMPANY BOSTON

1970

Published Simultaneously in Canada by

MCCLELLAND AND STEWART LIMITED

25 Hollinger Road, Toronto 374,
Ontario, Canada.

PRINTED AND BOUND IN ITALY

Contents

Author's Foreword

I T is well known, though not always acknowledged, that change is the one constant in all of life. We sometimes forget that change made possible all the living things we know. To students of birds, the most profound and dramatic change in the entire history of animals was the development of a reptile's scale into the feather of a bird. No one knows precisely when that happened, but it was something more than 140 million years ago. That is the approximate age of the oldest feather on record, a fossil imprint from the shale beds of Bavaria. It belonged to a strange creature called *Archaeopteryx* ("ancient wing").

Archaeopteryx was no ordinary bird. For one thing, it had teeth. Also, it had clawed fingers on its forelimbs and a long lizard-like tail with twenty vertebrae. But it was indisputably a bird, because by definition a bird is an animal with feathers. The change from *Archaeopteryx* onward has been brilliant and spectacular, but it all started with some little tree-clambering dinosaurs whose scales gradually changed into something much fancier to help sustain their lengthening leaps from branch to branch. In Darwin's words, "from so simple a beginning, endless forms most beautiful and wonderful have been, and are being evolved."

There is no way of knowing how many different kinds of birds evolved. Expert opinion is divided, but a round figure of one million is reasonable. Of these only a small fraction have ever co-existed at any one time. At present there are between eight and nine thousand species of birds in the world; in North America we have about seven hundred and seventy-five. Such an assemblage is unwieldy for the student, and long ago biologists began to sort out animals into groups of obviously related species. Clearly an ostrich is in a different group from a hummingbird or an owl or a thrush. The result is that the list of birds of the world is broken down under twenty-eight major headings called "orders," of which we have nineteen in North America. Of these by far the largest is the order "Passeriformes," which includes more than half the species of birds on earth.

All the birds in this volume are members of the order Passeriformes ("perching birds"). Many other kinds of birds can and do perch (herons, hawks, kingfishers, and many more), but they do not belong to this group. In general the perchers are the smaller birds, the ones we usually call "songbirds" regardless of the quality of their voices. The only members of this order in Volume I were the flycatchers and the swallows.

The perching birds are relatively recent arrivals, in an evolutionary sense. Warblers, vireos, tanagers, blackbirds, and finches are so new, in fact, that it is sometimes difficult to decide just who belongs to what family (the yellow-breasted chat is an excellent example). This problem is especially troublesome in the American tropics, where all of these seem to overlap to at least some extent, and where a number of birds do not seem to have yet "made up their minds" whether they are going to become one thing or another. Change is still very much with us.

Some of our most familiar birds are still in the process of busily subdividing into something else. Most of us know a song sparrow, but *the* song sparrow is impossible to define, as north of Mexico there are over thirty different geographic races, or sub-species, of the bird. Each is potentially a new species. So in looking at the various "kinds" of song sparrows we are actually witnessing new species on the assembly line. We are seeing the process of evolutionary change.

There is no question that of all the changes our planet has seen, none has taken place so quickly as those brought about by technological man. Some have had unexpectedly wide ramifications. In 1967, in the process of writing Volume I, I mentioned the dangers presented by the transference of the residues of chemical pesticides from prey species to predatory birds. "This is happening in our generation among peregrine falcons, bald eagles, and ospreys, all of which are seriously declining in numbers, as the result of ingesting toxic chemicals with their food." What I was unable to say was *how* it was happening; at that time we did not know. The circumstantial evidence was there, but positive identification of the poisoning mechanism was lacking. How did DDT and other pesticides affect the birds?

Now we know. Almost coincident with the publication of Volume I in the fall of 1968 there came firm clinical proof of the relationship between chlorinated hydrocarbon insecticides and bird reproduction. Experiments conducted with captive sparrow hawks by the U.S. Bureau of Sport Fisheries and Wildlife showed that repeated small doses of the poisons had the effect of altering enzyme balances in the birds' livers. In turn this affected the birds' sex hormones, such as oestrogen. This resulted in changes in the birds' calcium metabolism: their eggs had shells which were so thin or insubstantial that they could not be incubated without breaking, or would not permit the proper development of the embryo. The decline in numbers of the peregrine falcon has been catastrophic; it has been followed by similar trends in the bald eagle and the brown pelican, among others. The kind of change brought about by widespread environmental degradation is the kind we would happily do without.

Whether "human nature" can change is another matter. It seems to me that if a day ever comes when we cannot enjoy and value and take steps to protect birds for their own sakes, without reference to our own interests, we will be in grave trouble. On a television program in 1969, Lamont Cole, the distinguished ecologist of Cornell University, said to me somewhat sadly that he had "pretty nearly given up trying to promote conservation on the grounds of aesthetics." That is a melancholy thought, and although I am forced to agree, I continue to hope most fervently that it will not always reflect the true state of our civilized condition.

In the last half-dozen years there has developed an acute public awareness of the precarious state of the human environment. It didn't come a moment too soon. Now, perhaps steps will be taken to alleviate the condition of the living world as a whole. I suppose we who value nature can take some comfort from the expectation that as long as people are still around, the planet will be habitable for birds. The converse, presumably, is also true.

There follow profiles of sixty selected "songbirds" which are characteristic of the deciduous and mixed forests of the east, and of the open farmlands within it. It is hoped that the reader will now become more aware of some of the smaller and sometimes less conspicuous but usually quite common birds of our own man-made environment. Most of them have at least to some extent made their peace with human settlements and habitations, and almost all (at least in migration) can be seen within the limits of the typical eastern city. For a full description of the nature of the area under discussion, the reader is referred to the Introduction to Volume I.

A writer's life is fraught with complications. When there are deadlines to meet and potential conflicts to sort out, the survival of both project and author is to a great extent governed by the patience and ingenuity of publisher, agent, editors, and co-workers. My gratitude is warmly expressed to M. F. Feheley, J. G. McClelland, Peter Smith, Judith Symons, Anna Szigethy, and Michael Worek.

John A. Livingston

The work in this book owes much to the help of several people. The names of some of them have been mentioned in previous volumes, and if I do not repeat them now, my gratitude for their assistance has not diminished.

Most of the specimens used came from the Smithsonian Institution, through the kindness of Dr. S. Dillon Ripley who permitted me to keep more than a hundred skins for the two years it took me to do the paintings. As well, James L. Baillie, as he had done for years, chose and lent me fine skins from the Royal Ontario Museum whenever I needed them.

A difficulty ever-present in such works — that of finding the appropriate plants for the backgrounds — was greater in the case of this book. All the birds depicted on the following pages are small and spend their lives amid leaves and foliage not to be found on the West Coast where I work. Consequently, plants had to be shipped to me, and the office of picker and shipper of greens was filled by my friend Dudley Witney. Dudley showed incredible kindness, alacrity, and persistence in gathering the necessary things. Packages and boxes followed one another in a long procession to my door — each filled with carefully chosen, pressed, and labeled specimens, always quite fresh. I think Dudley must have spent months hunting, for many more plants came than I could possibly use.

The background of the Kentucky warblers was airmailed to me in an open carton, complete with insects and leaf-mould. Far from its Ontario woodlot home, this microcosmos went through its year of flowering and seeding. Now, still intact, it is sunk in the soil of my garden.

It may never notice the change.

J. Fenwick Lansdowne

plate 53—the sketch

BLUE JAY

Cyanocitta cristata

plate 53 BLUE JAY *Cyanocitta cristata*

*I*T is difficult to be indifferent to the crow family; all of them are noisy, conspicuous, aggressive, intelligent, and overflowing with personality. Audubon, never a man to let emotion go unexpressed, railed against the blue jay in particular, calling it a rogue, a thief, and a knave; he charged the bird with mischief, selfishness, duplicity, and even malice – words we usually reserve for creatures higher on the evolutionary scale. Audubon did concede, however, that the jay was a beautiful and cheerful bird and, by this qualification, joined the rest of us interested, delighted, and baffled by the cavalier behaviour of a bird which ranges from Alberta to Newfoundland, from Texas to Florida.

The facts, however, bear out very few of the many charges made against the blue jay. The blue jay will eat almost anything that is edible, but when, occasionally, it takes the eggs or chicks of another species, moralists should remember that the economy of nature stacks rather heavy odds against a young bird's survival. Ornithologists have estimated, furthermore, that a good three-quarters of a jay's food is vegetable, especially corn and cereal grains and acorns.

To deal with an acorn, a jay will hold the nut in its feet and crack it with its straight, strong bill. Jays are known frequently to bury acorns in the ground and, whether or not they ever find all of them, they thus help seed the oak forest.

In the early days, the blue jays were, no doubt, confined to the beech and oak woodlands which at that time provided most of their food. The birds have adjusted readily to the growth of cities and suburbs and are now common wherever there are suitable stands of trees. I, for example, have a boyhood memory of a jay's bulky, untidy nest in a slender ash just outside my bedroom window, in the heart of Toronto. I remember being surprised that the three-week-old fledglings, apart from the shortness of their still-growing tails, were almost indistinguishable from the adults.

Blue jays are uncharacteristically quiet during nesting time, but when the young are out and flying, families of them begin to make the racket we have learned to expect from this very garrulous tribe. The parties become larger as units of families drift together, and the din they make over a prowling house cat can be heard for blocks.

The jays' autumn flocking coincides with the appearance of the various nuts, berries, and fruits upon which the birds gorge as they gradually move southward.

There are few places better than Point Pelee National Park for watching a blue jay migration. The birds drift in a generally southwest direction in smallish, gradually merging groups; when they arrive at the southwest corner of Lake Erie, the individual flocks run into the hundreds. Taverner recalled a famous blue jay flight at Point Pelee on October 14, 1906. I have seen a good many, the greatest of which was on September 19, 1968, when at least three thousand jays passed overhead. James Baillie estimated at the time that they outnumbered the sharp-shinned hawks (always a feature at Pelee in the fall) by three to one.

Despite this massive migration, blue jays are with us all year. Local populations seem to shift southward during the winter, and, except in the South, the birds seen at that season are not usually the ones seen at breeding time. Their often tyrannical behaviour at feeding stations, to which they are easily attracted by peanuts and other seeds, probably helps to harm the jays' reputation. I have noticed that house sparrows and starlings almost invariably give way before the blue despot, but I have seen a jay and a male cardinal feeding (apparently amicably) side by side, with a few sturdy evening grosbeaks fluttering in from time to time without any undue disturbance.

Length 10 inches. Female, Haliburton County, Ontario, September 3.

plate 54—the sketch

COMMON CROW
Corvus brachyrhynchos

plate 54

COMMON CROW *Corvus brachyrhynchos*

BLACK is an unfortunate colour for a large, omnivorous bird. Whatever redeeming traits the crow may have (and it has many), the bird's very blackness seems to condemn it. Few native animals have been persecuted with such savage persistence. In winter, crows often roost together in enormous flocks. These flocks may include tens or even scores of thousands of individuals who, one way and another, managed to elude the guns and poisoned baits set out earlier in the season. Then comes the most frightful onslaught of all: crow killers actually bomb the roosts with dynamite.

These witless, offensive measures against the crow are taken in the name of "control" – a widely used euphemism for wanton destruction of a species which does not happen to be protected by law. There is no blood-thirstiness like that of the self-righteous. Allegations against the crow have traditionally come from the duck hunters, who claim that the bird has a bad effect on the production of waterfowl they want to shoot; but these allegations have no basis in fact. Farmers also used to hate crows but, in latter years, they seem to be realizing that flocks of crows can be decidedly beneficial by devouring crop-destroying insects. Some "sportsmen," however, have achieved a certain notoriety by inventing sophisticated methods of luring crows to their guns, even resorting to tape-recorded assembly calls of the birds.

The standard "put-down" among birdwatchers is the question "Do you know the crow?" It is assumed that everyone knows the crow, and indeed almost everyone does, no matter where he lives. But the crow is a thoroughly uncommon animal. Large, strong, resourceful, and apparently cunning, it has withstood with notable success the best-organized and largest-scale onslaughts its persecutors have yet been able to devise. The crow continues to thrive.

In the latitude of the Great Lakes, the March migration of the crows is one of the most stirring events of the year. Long, loose skeins of birds in flight move along lakeshores and over empty, barren fields, fighting blustery winds all the way. From their occasional, raucous *caws* one might even believe that they were enjoying the whole thing to the fullest. When the flocks arrive on their breeding grounds, they stick together for a time, feeding sociably. Then the pairs gradually break off and become solitary quiet for the nesting period.

A crow's nest, usually well hidden in an evergreen, is large and somewhat awkward looking. It is well constructed, however, and withstands the effects of the elements so well that last year's crows' nests are frequently used by hawks and owls with a minimum of refurbishing. There are about five greenish eggs, usually spotted with browns or grays. The young birds eat exclusively animal matter (mostly insects and other invertebrates), but on a year-round basis, vegetable matter forms almost three-quarters of the birds' intake.

The crow's fondness for corn is well known. In winter, standing corn is its favourite place for gathering, feeding, and sheltering. The birds, it seems, are blessed with adaptability and a high degree of survival potential, and have benefited from wide stretches of agricultural land. They take not only the corn but also many of the small mammals which frequent such places – including mice, voles, and shrews.

Crows will also visit and even take up temporary residence around the breeding colonies of birds such as herons and gulls. If the nesting birds are not disturbed, the impact of the black hangers-on is minimal. The only significant predation by crows on colonial birds that I have witnessed takes place when curious people put the sitting birds off their nests. Then the crows move in swiftly, silently, and efficiently. In such cases, we would be wise to reserve judgement.

Length 18 inches. Male, Wells Gray Park, British Columbia, May 14.

J.F. LANSDOWNE
·1969·
Corvus brachyrhynchos ♂
Horse Creek, Wells Gray Park, B.C.
May 14th, 1958   no. 10951
B.C. Prov. Mus.

plate 55 — the sketch

BLACK-CAPPED CHICKADEE
Parus atricapillus

plate 55 # BLACK-CAPPED CHICKADEE *Parus atricapillus*

CHICKADEES are year-round features of most of our range, tending to shift southward in winter. Some years their movements are more marked than usual. Very occasionally there is a chickadee flight large enough to constitute an "irruption," but irruptions are exceptional. In the non-breeding season we usually see parties of chickadees moving about in a somewhat aimless manner, often in company with other small birds such as kinglets and, in the migration period, warblers.

It is in the winter that we know the chickadee best. It appears to be the most fearless of our birds. Rare is the suet that does not attract a party of these hardy mites; with a little patience one can even encourage them to come to hand. There are few bird journals or family magazines which have not at one time or another shown photographs of children more or less festooned with these "cheerful" little birds.

The fiercest weather does not seem to bother them. This is a matter of physiology. Compared to a man, a bird is internally a raging inferno. The chickadee's heart, for example, beats five hundred times a minute when the bird is *asleep* and about twice that when it is exercising. This, compared to our sluggardly, near-reptilian seventy to eighty beats a minute, is a good indication why a small bird must eat almost constantly just to stay alive. Cold does not bother a winter bird; lack of food does. If the fires are kept supplied with fuel, the bird's high-powered metabolism – plus layers of loose, fluffy, insulating feathers – keep it going.

The chickadee is famous for its hyper-active way of feeding. In its search for the various invertebrates which make up its diet – insects and spiders, their egg masses and cocoons – it does all sorts of acrobatics. It hangs upside down, flutters and dances about, and adopts any number of strange and unlikely postures. Its sharp little bill can penetrate the most difficult and narrow cracks and crevices. Occasionally the bird will peck, almost like a woodpecker.

In the spring, breeding pairs of chickadees seem to be made up before the birds' final territories are declared. In the process, there is much chasing about, as the birds dart around the chosen area. Both sexes work at excavating the nesting hole (usually in an old and rotten stump, often that of a birch) jabbing vigorously at the pulpy, soft interior. They have little difficulty in digging and penetrate surprisingly sound wood.

The female may lay as many as ten eggs. (A small, vulnerable bird must have a high reproductive potential.) She does all the incubating, and, during those twelve days, the male brings food to her at the nest. Both share the duty of feeding the voracious young birds which will leave the nest after just a little over two weeks. The young, when they fly, are almost perfect replicas of the adults, except that they are somewhat scruffier.

Once they are out of the nest, young chickadees are quite competent to take care of themselves. This is where the chickadee's great agility comes into play. High-speed photographs have shown that when a flying chickadee is suddenly startled, it can react and begin to take evasive action within three one-hundredths of a second. You would expect this lightning response to be sufficient to protect it from most avian predators – which are so often notoriously inefficient – but I have seen a chickadee taken in mid-flight by a singularly nimble sparrow hawk.

The only species with which this bird can be confused is the very similar but more southern Carolina chickadee, which is somewhat smaller and grayer. The black-capped chickadee is thought to be the same species as the European willow tit; the phrase *tit-willow* is not included in the repertoire of either. The common call from which this bird gets its name is known to everyone. The so-called "spring" song, *phoebe,* can be heard at any season, and it is reported that "sixteen different vocalizations" have been listed.

Length 4¹/₂ inches.   Male, Haliburton County, Ontario, September 4.

plate 56—the sketch

TUFTED TITMOUSE
Parus bicolor

plate 56

TUFFED TITMOUSE *Parus bicolor*

THE family of titmice is a large one; about sixty diminutive species are scattered over all the continents of the world, except South America and Antarctica. For such tiny creatures, their dispersal has been impressive; they are thought to have originated in Eurasia, upwards of forty million years ago. "Tit" is an old Anglo-Saxon word for something very small; in Britain they still use the word for the birds we know as chickadees.

In North America, we have fourteen representatives of this attractive family. Those species with crests, of which we have four (there is only one in Europe), we call titmice; those without, we call chickadees. Crested or uncrested, they all belong to the genus *Parus*. There are others – the bushtits (*Psaltriparus*) and the verdin (*Auriparus*) of the West – which have branched off somewhat from the ancestral family stem.

Although it is a common bird in the eastern United States, the tufted titmouse rarely manages to enter Canada, in extreme southern Ontario. It was first recorded in Canada in 1914, and although there have been occasional very local indications of some increase, its success has been tentative at best. The progress of the tufted titmouse stands in marked contrast to that of the cardinal, also originally a southerner, which has made such a spectacular northward advance in this century. Both birds are the same in one respect, however: both are non-migratory, and when they do establish themselves, they stay the year round, despite the climate.

The titmouse is a plain but subtly attractive little bird. Its generally gray colour, its crest, and its brown flanks are to be watched for. One of its best field marks is the surprisingly conspicuous black, beady eye, which contrasts brightly with the otherwise "mousy" plumage. The sexes look similar. Like any other chickadee, the titmouse is extremely active in its feeding, and does all the charming acrobatics characteristic of the family. Caterpillars are said to be regarded as a delicacy by titmice, and the birds depend all year chiefly on the eggs, larvae, and pupae of insects. In the appropriate season they are also known to eat beechnut mast and acorns.

Titmice seem to prefer dense hardwoods, with the forest floor dampish to downright wet. They will, however, come to residential areas if there is a sufficient number of large shade trees. They are not difficult to attract to bird feeders at any season; when we Canadians receive one of our rare glimpses of a titmouse, it is usually at a feeding station. (I have had my most intimate acquaintance with the bird at the attractive feeder maintained by the Roger Petersons in Connecticut.) In time, and with patience, the bird can be made to come to hand like a black-capped chickadee.

Titmice nest in cavities, natural and artificial. Often they are said to use old woodpecker holes. The one nest I have seen was in a bird box a little over eye level in a deep New Jersey woodland. (The box appeared to be crammed to overflowing with soft material.) There are usually about five or six eggs. In fall and winter the titmice associate in small flocks with other resident, non-migratory birds. During migration they frequently mingle with myrtle warblers.

Probably the most distinctive feature of the titmouse is its voice. It will call at any time of the year, and, at any distance, its loudly whistled three-note phrases will remind you of the Carolina wren or, possibly, of the cardinal. You can easily attract the bird to you by squeaking or by imitating its call – not a difficult one.

Length 5¹/₂ inches.   Female, Amelia Island, Florida, October 15.

plate 57 — the sketch

WHITE-BREASTED NUTHATCH
Sitta carolinensis

plate 57 # WHITE-BREASTED NUTHATCH *Sitta carolinensis*

BIRDS like crows and jays have made a great success of being "generalized." They can eat almost anything, and they obtain their food in almost as many ways as there are items in their diet. Under the right circumstances, however, it has paid some birds to be highly specialized. The world's fifteen species of nuthatches, of which we have four in North America, have managed to make the best of a style of survival which is uniquely their own.

When you see a bird which habitually clings upside-down to the bark of large trees, it is a nuthatch. There is one other species, the red-breasted, within the geographic scope of this book; it is slightly smaller, and has a black line through the eye. The more southern, white-breasted bird is identifiable by its size and its pure white cheek patch.

Nuthatches are characterized by their sturdy, "neckless" bodies and strong, tapered bills. The tail is short, the wings relatively long. The toes are quite long to assist in bark-clinging. One foot is usually braced at right angles to the body, the other pointed downward.

It has been suggested that nuthatches succeed in their upside-down approach to life because, in this way, they may spot food items that the more conventional, rightside-up creepers and woodpeckers might miss. It is true that forest insects in various stages of metamorphosis, and their eggs, are eaten by nuthatches, and this posture would be suitable for foraging, but a very high proportion of the birds' food is vegetable. (Anyone who operates a feeding station knows their fondness for sunflower seeds.) They will also take quantities of beechnuts and acorns, among a wide selection of berries and other fruits. To balance its winter diet, however, the nuthatch will vary its seed intake with quantities of suet. It has been known to come to salt.

A nuthatch opens nuts and hard seeds by breaking them open with the bill (hence the bird's name). It will attack a nut or seed on the ground or on your feeding tray; it will sometimes fly with it to a tree with good rough bark and lodge it there, and go about breaking it with hard strokes of its efficient beak. (Even if it is not hungry, it will continue to place nuts and seeds in the bark of trees; this "cache" may or may not be remembered later.) The bird has been known to forage on the ground.

Nuthatches are with us all year, but they are most conspicuous in winter, when they show little fear around our houses and their voices are among the very few bird sounds we hear. The familiar *yank, yank* is supplemented by various other calls we hear less often. The song is described by Godfrey as a hollow whistled *tew, tew, tew, tew*. In winter nuthatches are often accompanied by creepers, chickadees, and downy woodpeckers.

In spring courtship, the male pursues the female in mad, careening chases. The birds show great agility in the air, and good speed when they pass overhead, but they rarely fly far. They nest in a cavity in a tree – sometimes a natural rotten spot or knothole, sometimes a woodpecker hole. The birds will sometimes use a bird box, but they are perfectly capable of excavating their own premises, if need be. Look for them in oak and maple woods with plenty of decaying old trees (the kind of stands that economics-minded foresters delight in calling "over-mature"). The nest is softly lined with fine fibres, bits of wool or hair, and feathers. The male will feed the female as part of the courtship ritual, and will indulge in whatever strutting and posturing his upside-down position allows. The nuthatch is a fecund bird, producing ten or even more eggs, but the average is probably eight. Both sexes take care of the young, which look just like their parents when they emerge.

The white-breasted nuthatch is found over most of the United States and in Mexico, but is more scattered in Canada. It occurs in southern British Columbia, southeastern Manitoba, and the St. Lawrence Valley – rarely on the prairies.

Length 5 inches.   Male, Laurel, Maryland, October 8.

plate 58—the sketch

BROWN CREEPER
Certhia familiaris

plate 59—the sketch

HOUSE WREN
Troglodytes aedon

plate 59 HOUSE WREN *Troglodytes aedon*

THE wren family is of American origin. Of all the fifty-nine species of wrens in this hemisphere, only one has ventured to the Old World, where our winter wren has become "Jenny." Although the house wren has not followed its relative across the Bering Strait, it has spread (assuming its Central and South American counterpart to be the same species) from central Canada to Tierra del Fuego. A bewildering number of subspecific races have been recognized, but to all intents and purposes they are all house wrens.

Wrens are among the most volatile of birds, and the house wren is the most vigorous, aggressive, and mercurial of them all. Almost everyone knows a wren, and almost everyone knows this one, which has used man and his buildings to its fullest advantage. It readily accepts artificial nesting boxes, sometimes at the expense of other small birds, such as bluebirds, which we may want to attract.

The spring migration of house wrens goes almost unnoticed. One does not see flocks of them moving along, as in the case of so many other species. But on a bright spring morning, the bubbling, tempestuous song breaks out – and the tyrant of the backyard has arrived. As he sits on a fence, his throat and whole body quivering with the intensity of his song, the bird seems on the point of exploding with energy and emotion. Singing almost without pause, he forthwith begins to build a nest – or several of them – which may be in varying stages of completion when the females arrive.

During the nesting period, wrens are hard on other wrens, and even on birds of other species. They have been justly accused of scolding and chivvying larger birds, puncturing their eggs, killing their young and even the adults. (The house wren himself is known to have been evicted – by his cousin, the Carolina wren.) It almost seems that the wren's territorial urge is inversely proportioned to his size; he cannot tolerate anything with feathers near his nesting site.

Although we are most accustomed to thinking of wrens using bird houses, some bizarre sites have been recorded. Audubon placed his house wren family in an old felt hat, and said he had seen "many" in such quarters. Other unlikely nesting sites listed by Gross in Bent's *Life Histories* include a fish creel, watering pot, tin can, farm implements, teapots, a soap dish, boots and shoes, weathervanes, a coat pocket, and on the "rear axle of an automobile which was used daily." Gross says, "When the car was driven the wrens went along." They even hatched the eggs. No creature this adaptable could have failed to succeed.

A house wren's nest is typically a large, messy assortment of twigs and little sticks jammed into whatever space is available. As he may build several nests, he is kept frantically busy. Gross notes, "While so employed he often acquires a second mate while the first is still busy with household duties." Polygamy is fairly common with the house wren. In many cases, mates separate after the first brood. In fact, the female may already be looking for a second mate while her first brood is still in the nest, and the male is stuck with raising the fledglings.

There are a lot of house wrens; they nest twice, and the usual number of eggs is six or eight. It follows that there must be a very high mortality rate among the young, or we would have house wrens at pest proportions. Ninety percent or even more fail to reach breeding age. This is an excellent example of how nature ensures an inventory upon which to draw should there be a "crash" of adult house wrens. Otherwise, natural mortality keeps replacement at about par. A brutal method, perhaps, but utterly effective.

It is interesting that, as early as 1925, E. C. Hoffman noticed the adverse effects of pesticides on house wrens. He reported dead nestlings in abandoned nests in three successive years at a time when currant bushes were dusted with arsenate of lead. The adults disappeared shortly after they had carried arsenate-covered green currant worms to the nest. The pest control methods of forty-five years ago were primitive by comparison with the subtle synthetic compounds of today.

Length 4¹/₂ inches.   Male, Washington, D.C., September 23.

plate 60—the sketch

CAROLINA WREN
Thryothorus ludovicianus

plate 60 # CAROLINA WREN *Thryothorus ludovicianus*

WRENS being the cautious, somewhat secretive creatures they are, chances are one will hear several Carolina wrens (and sometimes wonder whether they are titmice or cardinals) for every one seen. Its loud, rich carol has a rhythmic, rollicking nature which is characteristic: the song is usually a spirited three-part *tea-kettle, tea-kettle,* or a two-part *wheedle, wheedle* repeated half a dozen times. The song rings through the damp hardwood forests with authority and clarity at all seasons of the year. There are sundry variations, too, and a rich assortment of scolding, chattering notes.

The largest member of its family in the East is clearly identifiable as a wren by its shape and cocked-tail posture. The rich rufous upperparts and warm buffy underparts, together with a conspicuous eye-stripe, are unique. The Carolina wren is a sturdy-looking bird, perceptibly chunkier than its relatives. It is not common in Canada (where it is restricted to southern Ontario), but it occupies almost all of the eastern United States.

The bird is more aptly named than some, as it is unquestionably a southern animal, but in this century it has gradually pioneered its way northward, as have both the cardinal and, to a lesser extent, the tufted titmouse. It is sedentary and non-migratory, so wherever it happens to arrive in the north, there it will probably stay for the winter. The fact that it does not return to a more salubrious climate in the colder months has no doubt slowed its invasion of the North, but it now appears to have taken a reasonably firm hold along the north shores of Lakes Erie and Ontario.

Like all wrens, this bird is a confirmed "skulker"; it prefers dense, very brushy thickets. However, it will upon occasion become somewhat more confident and, especially in the South, it is often a familiar dooryard bird. It will even use buildings and other structures for nesting purposes; but it will do so only if there is good dense cover close by, into which it can retreat and angrily scold the passer-by. In a state of nature, the Carolina wren sticks to rich, wet woods, always with deep, tangled undergrowth.

The nest is rather large and looks somewhat informal from the outside, as so many wrens' nests do; the inner lining is composed of whatever soft materials are available. If it is forced to build in the open, the bird will often roof the nest over with a dome, with an opening in the side. As is the case with the house wren, the female is thought to incubate, but the final rearing of the young is often left to the male. Two or three broods are common in the south, each with from four to six young.

Birds as energetic, aggressive, and prolific as wrens commonly become involved in nuptial tangles. A. R. Laskey gave an interesting account in *Bird-Banding* of nest-building behaviour gone awry. A male Carolina wren became interested in a neighbourhood female and began to build a nest as part of his courtship ritual. Unfortunately he chose for its site the nest in which the female of his choice, and her mate, were already raising a brood of young. The parents kept on feeding the young birds despite the growing pile of twigs and other debris on top of them. The interloper was eventually removed a sufficient distance, and the brood was raised successfully.

Like most of our wrens, the Carolina is chiefly insectivorous, although in winter it will resort to a few seeds and berries. It will also come to your backyard feeding station. For those of us in the north to whom this is an uncommon species, feeders usually provide some of our best glimpses of the bird. It will not accept the offerings unless there is a deep tangled thicket somewhere close at hand, into which it may pop at an instant's notice. It is a curious bird and, even when it is in the depths of its retreat, it cannot restrain itself from coming forth to investigate the squeaking noises every birdwatcher learns to make. But it won't stay out long; its curiosity satisfied (or its attention span exhausted), it will again flit out of sight.

Length 4³/₄ inches.   Male, Statesville, North Carolina, October 6.

plate 61—the sketch

MOCKINGBIRD
Mimus polyglottos

plate 61 MOCKINGBIRD *Mimus polyglottos*

A BIRDWATCHER learns to expect the unexpected, but the experience of Gerry Bennett at Petrolia, Ontario, near Windsor, richly deserves recording. It took place quite a number of years ago, at a time when Bennett had never seen a mockingbird. In the course of a morning's outing, he discovered a strange nest which was quite new to him. Baffled, he made a detailed description of nest and eggs, and on his next visit to the Royal Ontario Museum, he learned that he had found one of the then extremely rare Canadian nests of the mockingbird. A year or so later Bennett added the mockingbird to his personal list.

Mockingbirds are rarely seen in Canada. When one remembers that this elegant and personable species has been chosen the state bird of Arkansas, Florida, Mississippi, Tennessee, and Texas, one knows where to go to see it in its proper context. It was on my first visit to Texas, appropriately enough, that I first realized the mocker would sing all night long.

The song is the thing; the most eloquent and impassioned of American bird writers have striven to say the unspeakable. The mockingbird is, to be sure, an indefatigable singer, rather like the storied nightingale (which to my ear is more to be admired for the persistence of its rapid, disjointed, and extremely repetitive phrases than for euphony). As his name *Mimus polyglottos* (mimic of many tongues) implies, the mocker repeats the songs and calls of other birds. Many and remarkable have been the recorded feats of its mimicry. One or two examples will suffice. One "imitated thirty-two different kinds of birds in a space of ten minutes." Another is reported to have changed his tune eighty-seven times in seven minutes. Yet another changed one hundred and thirty-seven times in ten minutes. One of the most famous of all was said to imitate thirty-nine bird songs and fifty bird calls, plus the notes of a frog and a cricket. As Alexander Sprunt Jr. observes in Bent's *Life Histories* (source of the above records), the word for the mocker is "matchless."

The bird is, without question, matchless as a mimic. And it has delightful notes of its own. I think this is the most admirable bird we have – not only to listen to but also to watch. It sings from a very conpicuous perch, whether a telephone pole, a wire, or naked branch of a tree. But it soon stops singing when its year-round territorial prerogatives are threatened. No one transgresses the borders of a mocker's plot. He will fly fiercely at any other mockingbird and chase it away. He will chivvy cats and dogs – and people. He will "see off" birds of any species.

One winter evening, in a Florida garden, I saw the mockingbird's temper tested beyond reason. A very large flock of more than two hundred robins descended for food, drink, and bathing. The resident mockingbird was having fits as he attempted to drive them away. His rage and frustration mounted to terrible intensity; he flew repeatedly at the robins who came close to his favorite corner. He did manage to keep clear one small patch of lawn about thirty feet square, and within that area the robins appeared to defer to him. (I could not escape the anthropomorphic notion that the bigger birds were simply humouring him.) He was the picture of outraged fury, of course, and perhaps from a robin's eye view he may have appeared very fierce indeed.

The mockingbird is a slender, well-kept bird. It appears somewhat nondescript at rest – its most conspicuous feature being the long tail. Occasionally, a ruffle of feathers will reveal a pale highlight. In flight, however, the mocker becomes a different bird altogether, with flashing white patches in wings and tail.

The mocker does a good deal of foraging on the ground, poking for insects, picking up small fruits, and so on. It follows that a good number of the territorial incidents in the bird's life take place at ground level. Tails raised, heads tautly erect, the birds will face each other stiffly. They may hop about and then take to the air, one hotly pursuing the other. Or they may both go their own ways, their obligations satisfactorily concluded.

Length 9 inches.   Male, Havana, Cuba, February 21.

plate 62—the sketch

CATBIRD
Dumetella carolinensis

plate 62 # CATBIRD *Dumetella carolinensis*

I AM unmoveably persuaded that the catbird was placed upon this earth solely for the instruction and delight of small boys. It is common. Its voice is varied and attractive. It is secretive enough to provoke curiosity. Its nest is difficult to find (but not *too*). Its eggs are among the most handsome of any of the more common species. Sighting a catbird can recall almost-forgotten scents of spring lilacs, honeysuckles, and mock-oranges – the mysteries of dense Chinese elm hedges, hawthorn thickets, and hillside sumac groves.

This is the smallest of our eastern mimics (continentally, only the sage thrasher of the West is smaller), and the darkest. To all intents and purposes, it is a slate-gray bird with no remarkable features. Only on quite close inspection do you notice the black cap, and, on rather exceptional occasions, have a glimpse of the chestnut colouring under the tail. Usually the bird is in low silhouette against the sky or deep in the shadows of some thicket, even when it is singing at its best. Notice the slender shape and the long, flirting tail. It will occasionally emerge in response to your squeaks, but will quickly retire to its covert again.

The song of the catbird is not as varied as the mockingbird's, and it does not repeat its phrases. (Remember that the mockingbird makes many repetitions without pause, and that the brown thrasher speaks in couplets.) The catbird is every bit as musical as the mocker, however, and its own notes and phrases always take precedence over a rather minor degree of mimicry. The call note, the catlike *mew* which gives the bird its name, is often thrown into the pattern of the complete song. At the height of the season, this is one of the several species which will sing at night. A gentle, quiet "whisper song" has been noted in the autumn.

Under natural circumstances the catbird likes to nest in brushy, overgrown openings in the woods, shrubby meadows, and tangled ancient orchards. Run-down farmlands are ideal, in fact. Urban situations can be to its liking as long as there is plenty of dense shrubbery. There is every likelihood that an increase in this kind of habitat since settlement of the continent has been reflected in an increase in the catbird population. You will never find the bird in thick woods.

Although birds of this family have a tendency to stay close to their favourite singing perches, and not to move around much in the nesting season, when they do decide to move they are surprisingly swift and darting in their actions. This is particularly noticeable during courtship chases, when the male pursues the female across the lawn, in and out of the shrub borders, with a flickering speed that is quite unexpected.

The nest is large, and coarse-looking on the outside – a jumble of small sticks and twigs. But it is neatly lined within, with various soft materials. There is an average of four deep blue-green eggs, much darker than those of a robin, with an unusual glossy look to them – most beautiful. There are usually two broods, and the birds may or may not have the same mates the second time around. Catbirds' nests are occasionally parasitized by the cowbird, and sometimes the yellow-billed cuckoo has been known to contribute an egg to the catbird's clutch.

Catbird food is as varied as that of the other mimics; in season, various fruits and berries are important. In the south, there have been some allegations of serious catbird depredations on berry crops, but this seems to be of no significance in our area. In spring and summer, when young are being raised, the birds consume vast quantities of insects and other invertebrates, with emphasis on beetles and caterpillars of many kinds.

Most catbirds winter in the southern United States and Central America; the occasional individual roughs it out farther north.

Length 7³/₄ inches.   Male, Brandenburg, Kentucky, April 30.

plate 63—the sketch

BROWN THRASHER
Toxostoma rufum

plate 63 ## BROWN THRASHER *Toxostoma rufum*

OUR largest eastern mimic is also the most colourful and the most elusive. While mockingbirds and (to a lesser extent) catbirds commonly frequent our gardens and door-yards, the thrasher keeps chiefly to itself. It is not as common as the other two, but is by no means scarce. It is trite to say a bird is more often heard than seen, but the saying is particularly true of the brown thrasher.

The bird's spring song is one of the more pronounced features of the season. Choosing a conspicuous, reasonably high station, the male sings strongly and vigorously; his loud notes carry for good distances. Although all rules have their exceptions, the thrasher *generally* sings in couplets, repeating each phrase only once before it moves on to another. It makes identification quite easy. The bird does not go in for mimicry nearly as much as the mockingbird does, or even the catbird. One may see the male while one is still a long way from him – his head will be raised, his long tail hanging below. But he will not allow a close approach; as you move toward him, he will hastily glide down to a suitably dense bit of shrubbery, there anxiously to await your passing. Photographs of singing thrashers are uncommon.

A brown thrasher can only be confused in the East with a large thrush, but it is much longer – by almost two inches – than any thrush. However, it does look superficially like one, and Audubon knew it as the "ferruginous thrush." His flamboyant plate illustrates three male thrashers, and a female, energetically defending a nest and four eggs against a black snake. In view of the strong territoriality of the thrasher, I have sometimes speculated about this plate, having in mind three adult males. But it is true that birds do tend to forget their internecine squabbles when there are dangerous predators around. And certainly the thrasher is dedicated in the defence of its plot. In any event, Audubon reported that the snake was finally done in, and that a "jubilee" was held over its carcass by a crowd of thrashers and other birds, "until the woods resounded with their notes of exultation"!

One's best look at a thrasher will probably come when it is foraging on the ground, as it commonly does. It is a long, tapered bird, bright cinnamon-rufous, with a graceful tail and a long, curved bill. At close quarters its gleaming yellow eye is surprisingly prominent. The bird will probe in your lawn for insects and their larvae, and will also "thrash" about noisily in the leaf litter at woodland edges. Its preferred food is insects – about two thirds of the total intake – but like its relatives it is also fond of wild fruit, including sumac, some cultivated berries, and acorn mast.

Nesting is always near the ground, or actually on it, invariably under good shelter such as thorn bushes, brush piles, tangled vines, and the like. I have found the nest remarkably difficult to find in view of the size and brilliant colour of the bird when it chooses to reveal itself. There are usually four eggs, not especially noteworthy for their beauty, being pale bluish with spotted brown. Like the other mimics, thrashers are impeccably clean about the nest, removing the fecal sacs of their offsprings religiously. They raise two broods, and may form new pairs for the second nesting. Thrashers have been known to lay eggs in the nests of other birds from time to time, including cardinals, robins, and wood thrushes.

This is the only thrasher in eastern North America; there are seven others in the West. Our bird will occasionally winter in the North, but generally it withdraws to the southern States.

Length 10 inches.   Male, South Carolina, March 18.

plate 64—the sketch

ROBIN

Turdus migratorius

plate 64 ROBIN *Turdus migratorius*

*I*F the first British colonists on the east coast of this continent had looked a little more closely at this hefty bird with the brick-red underparts, they might have realized it is much more closely related to the European blackbird than to the little robin redbreast of their homeland – although both are members of the thrush family. Many thrushes are spotted; our robins betray family characteristics in the plumage of the young birds and in their typically musical and varied songs.

There are sixty-odd members of the genus *Turdus*, most of them in the Old World. I have seen "robins" of one kind and another from Alaskan bogs to equatorial African jungles and forests of the Andes. They are all quite similar in build, posture, and behaviour – though not necessarily in colour. You can find our North American bird in deserts, woodlands, and cities – and from seashores to the high Rockies. It is one of our most widely distributed and successful birds.

Very few people do not know the robin. It seems to be one bird that has taken advantage of man and his works. All our settlements and other built-up areas are filled with robins. It is difficult to imagine a city park or a residential area without these birds; even industrial communities have robins. Frequently robins nest in unexpected locations – in parking lots, machine yards, and junkpiles, as well as on houses. But even though they have in a sense become human "satellites," robins are not as presumptuous as pigeons, house sparrows, and starlings. The robin remains very much a wild bird.

No robin in good health is self-effacing: it is a loud, strident, and vociferous bird. In spring and early summer, its clear carolling may begin well before dawn; for the birdwatcher arising while it is still dark, the robin is usually the first bird on the day's list. When it is not singing, the spring robin seems to be shrilling and screaming – wild courtship chases weave through our gardens and over our lawns always with piercing cries.

Birds of this genus build substantial nests, well-cemented with mud, easily recognizable. It is such a well-executed structure that you wonder why robins so frequently build a new nest in a new territory for their second brood. Usually there are four eggs. The robin has often been used as an example of population dynamics in nature. If both broods of four were successful, and all survived, we would have ten robins in the autumn for the two we had in the spring. It has been calculated that if this process were to go on uninterrupted, with adults and young continuing to survive for a period of ten years, there would be something of the order of nineteen *million* robins from that first pair. Of course this does not happen. Songbirds fall prey to predators, to diseases, to food shortages, and so on. Once out of the nest, the life expectancy of a young robin averages about a year and a half.

A sufficient number of robins do survive, however, to allow it to remain one of the most abundant birds on the continent. You need only see some of the spectacular flocks in Florida during the winter to realize what tremendous numbers of these birds there are. In the area just north of the entrance to Everglades National Park it is commonplace to see flocks of several hundred – often thousands. When they are on their way north, in the spring, they often roost en route in incredible numbers.

The robin's fondness for fruits, both wild and cultivated, is well-known. Large flocks can be a decided nuisance, sometimes, to cherry growers. But the bird's tastes are wide, and flocks seldom concentrate on any one item for very long. When young are in the nest they must have animal protein, and the birds' diligent search for earthworms is familiar to everyone. Unfortunately, earthworms containing DDT (often from elm leaves which they have eaten) can pass on lethal doses to the robins which prey on them.

Length 8¹/₂ inches.   Male, Kershaw County, South Carolina, March 5.
Female, New Orleans, Louisiana, March 12.
Young, Victoria, British Columbia, May.

plate 65—the sketch

WOOD THRUSH
Hylocichla mustelina

plate 65 # WOOD THRUSH *Hylocichla mustelina*

No sound in nature rivals the spring song of the wood thrush. When you first hear the strong, deliberately paced, incredibly musical phrases floating through the fresh green understorey of the hardwood forest, it is *the* high point of the year. No description of the song is adequate. For purity and richness, only the notes of the most sensitive woodwind seem comparable. The hermit thrush is the great singer of the boreal forest; but in the South, the wood thrush is in a category all its own.

Song is of course one of the chief characteristics of the great world family of thrushes. There are over three hundred species, including some of the most accomplished vocalists of all birds – nightingale, song thrush, and European blackbird among them. Thrushes are almost cosmopolitan as a family, but most of them are in the temperate zone and tropics of the Old World, where it is presumed they originated. On our continent, the thrushes are all strong migrants – most of them exceptionally hardy birds. This species winters in Central America, as far south as Panama.

In Canada, the wood thrush breeds only in southern Ontario and the extreme southernmost parts of Quebec, but its nesting range in the United States includes almost all of the eastern half of the country. This is the commonest thrush in the eastern hardwoods, with the exception of the robin. The latter has made itself much more at home in cities and otherwise built-up and populated areas; but in some places I suspect that wood thrushes are beginning to turn up more frequently in suburban gardens and well-wooded city ravines.

This bird is very much more like a robin than it is like the other brown *Hylocichla* thrushes – the veery, Swainson's, and gray-cheeked. Many authorities are now of the opinion that the wood hrush should join the robin in the genus *Turdus*, or rather that it should be restored to that genus. It used to be known (probably quite correctly) as *Turdus mustelinus*. In addition to more subtle pieces of evidence, the wood thrush is built rather differently from the others – heftier and chunkier – more like a robin. Had I not seen the owner of the first wood thrush nest I ever found, I would certainly have assumed it was that of a robin. Wood thrush spring courtship displays and chases are very robin-like. On the other hand, the occasional robin virtuoso can manage to sound something like a wood thrush.

We do not often see numbers of wood thrushes in migration. Usually the first evidence of the birds' presence is their song. The male is said to begin singing early in the season from high treetops, then, as the spring progresses, gradually to move to lower levels of vegetation. Certainly when the nesting period is well under way, the bird usually sounds as though it is singing from the ground, or very close to it. The flute-like phrases seem to echo and re-echo through the spring forest in delectable variety. But when you approach too closely, a sputtered, explosive alarm-note terminates the song. It is difficult actually to see a wood thrush singing; I still look forward to that pleasure.

In their study of the song of the wood thrush, Donald J. Borror and Carl R. Reese carefully checked the recorded songs of twenty-five different birds – no two of them sang identical songs. Their findings bore out a contention that had long been made by Aretas A. Saunders, one of the pioneers in this field, that one can recognize an individual wood thrush by his song. Borror and Reese discovered that beauty is only one of the features of this bird's voice. The song is, as well, incredibly complicated. Our ears miss most of its subtlety, but vibralyzer graphs illustrate the bird's "remarkable vocal gymnastics."

Length 7 inches.   Male, Washington, D.C., May 3.

plate 66—the sketch

VEERY
Hylocichla fuscescens

plate 66   VEERY *Hylocichla fuscescens*

IRDS do not usually come to birdwatchers; if an observer wants to see them, he must seek them out. Fortunately, there are occasional exceptions. As this book was being written, I was cooped up with my typewriter one May morning, too well aware that migration was at its peak. The birdwatcher's fidgety wanderlust was compensated for to some extent by a torrential rainstorm – the first big thundershower of the season. The rain pelted down harder and harder, with the noise level rising rapidly, when it was suddenly and cleanly interrupted by the glorious voice of a veery. The bird was singing in the height of the downpour, just a few feet from my studio window – but many miles from wherever it would nest. This is not an isolated phenomenon; I have several times heard veerys singing in the middle of the city; the rain seems to encourage them.

Usually one will hear the veery at its best at dawn and dusk, although the bird will sing throughout the day at the right season, and under cool, shady conditions. Associations play a large part in one's enjoyment of bird song; the veery's voice is always accompanied in my imagination by the clicks and peeps of frogs, the winnowing of snipe, the chirping of woodcock, the trills of amorous toads. One thinks of alder swales, willow thickets, and the depths of moist woodlands – and of uncountable mosquitoes.

The veery is rather easy to identify by its smooth warm colour over-all. The wood thrush has a reddish head; the hermit thrush has a reddish tail; gray-cheeked and Swainson's thrushes are more olive on the upperparts.

Winsor Marrett Tyler, in Bent's *Life Histories*, called the voice of the veery "one of the strangest sounds in nature." It has a quality which is strangely unbirdlike and almost impossible to describe. Each phrase is delivered at a lower pitch than the last, giving the full, rich song the effect of spiralling down the scale. One can often identify a bird by the quality of its voice with more assurance than by what it actually says. The veery's song has a husky nature which is quite characteristic. The notes are pure, but the voice has rich overtones – a "body" which makes it especially appealing. The call note is also distinctive – a whistled *wheeo*, with the emphasis dropping at the end.

The veery spends most of its time on or near the ground, searching the leaf litter for insects. Like all thrushes it eats fruits when they are available. The bird is often difficult to see in the forest. Walking along, one may glimpse a slender rufous-brown shape which darts from one hiding place to the next, and that will be all. Or, remaining perfectly still, one may see the bird perched, absolutely immobile, on a low twig. It is gone again in a wink, but the loud call-note will confirm the observation.

A veery's nest is built either on the ground or very close to it, deep in the ferns and low-growing shrubs of the forest carpet. The eggs are blue, rather like those of the wood thrush but smaller. Veerys nest almost right across the northern United States and southern Canada, but they do not quite reach the West Coast. They always adhere to hardwoods and mixed forests. They winter in northern and central South America.

Length 6 inches.   Male, Cook County, Illinois, May 1.

plate 67 — the sketch

EASTERN BLUEBIRD
Sialia sialis

plate 67

EASTERN BLUEBIRD *Sialia sialis*

Fᴙᴏᴍ the earliest days of settlement, few birds have prompted such exclamations of admiration as the gentle bluebird (although, as the tree swallow has learned, the bluebird is no gentler than any other under territorial conditions). It is unquestionably the most beautiful of our thrushes, with only its two western cousins, the mountain and western bluebirds, rivalling its pure, lovely colour.

Despite its rather ethereal appearance and its vulnerability to a number of natural and unnatural enemies, the bluebird is an extraordinarily hardy species. It goes no farther south in winter than it must; there are many records of birds wintering in Canada. In the East, most of them winter in the Carolinas, and often considerably farther north than that. In spring in our latitudes, the bluebird's throaty warble is one of the first signs of the new season; it drifts downward from fresh March winds as a promise of something better in store.

The ideal habitat for bluebirds is somewhat open country with scattered old trees; an abandoned farm or homestead is ideal, especially if there is a decrepit orchard to go with it. In colonial times and thereafter, bluebirds thrived; there was an abundance of nesting sites in rotten fruit trees and such places. Toward the end of the nineteenth century, however, stern competition arrived in the form of the tough, adaptable, and aggressive house sparrow, imported from Europe. The sparrows began forthwith to dispossess the bluebirds. No sooner had this happened than there was a second invasion – this time the even larger and more competitive European starling.

Worst of all, at about the same time as these invasions we began to go in for "clean farming" – the cutting down or pruning of old fruit trees, the removal of rotten fenceposts, and their replacement with metal posts. This had its effects almost overnight. The birds were driven from what remained of their habitat by the introduced exotics and had fewer and fewer places to which they could retreat.

Because bluebirds winter in large numbers in surprisingly high latitudes, they are vulnerable to sudden changes in the weather. A late February or early March freeze can catch them already on migration, and heavy losses have been suffered in late winter cold-snaps. Under normal conditions, no doubt, the birds' population dynamics had become adjusted to these occasional set-backs, but the additional pressures on their nesting grounds made it increasingly difficult for them to maintain their numbers. All these trials combined to bring the eastern bluebird population to a dangerously low level only a very few years ago.

Now, something positive may be happening. It is perhaps too early and over-optimistic to say so, but it *seems* that the imported Dutch elm disease may be giving the bluebird an unexpected "break." Many parts of its range are now filled with dead elm trees, which are attracting insects and, thus, woodpeckers. Many of the latter have provided new nesting sites for the bluebirds. Also, in the East there is evidence that the house sparrow populations have levelled off, and that starlings too may have become stabilized. If this is so, the dead elms may well contribute substantially to the beginning of a bluebird recovery.

Where nesting sites have been scarce, bluebirds have been assisted in many places by artificial nesting boxes. Many bird clubs and conservation societies have made projects of the building and setting up of bird houses designed especially for bluebirds. But even then, the bluebirds are not immune to the apparently "spiteful" attacks of house wrens. Also, tree swallows like to use bluebird boxes (although, as reported in Volume I, bluebirds have been known to dispossess the swallows).

Length 5¹/₂ inches.   Male, Mt. Vernon, Kentucky, October 3.
Female, Baton Rouge, Louisiana, January 3.

plate 68—the sketch

BLUE-GRAY GNATCATCHER
Polioptila caerulea

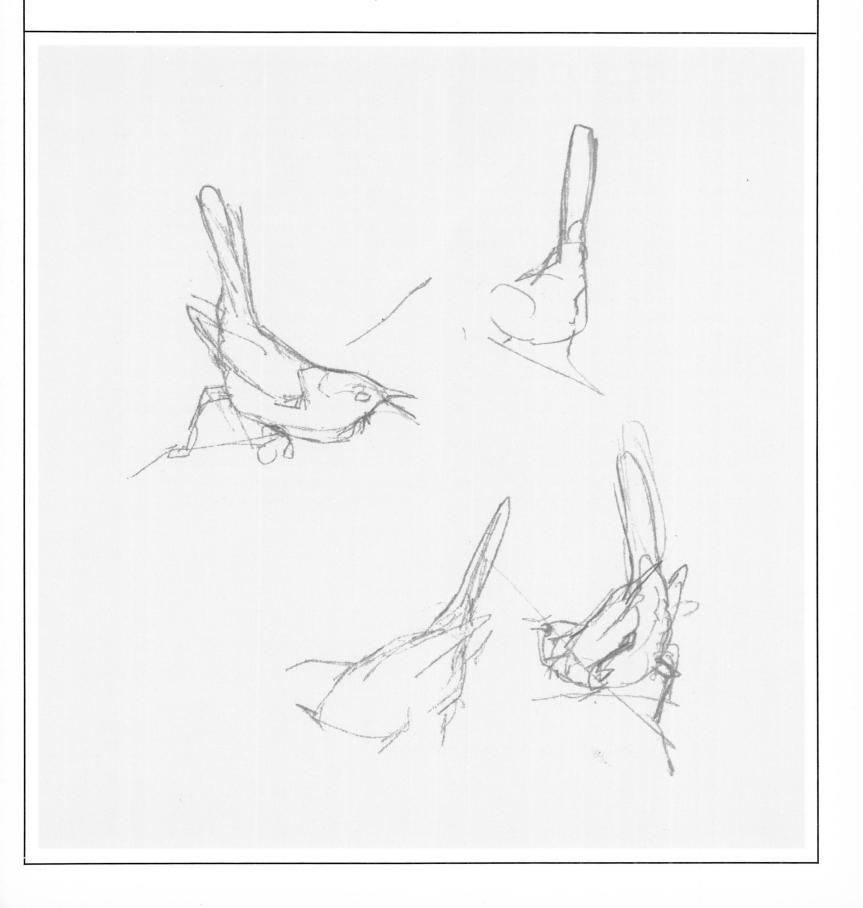

plate 68   # BLUE-GRAY GNATCATCHER *Polioptila caerulea*

GNATCATCHERS are treetop feeders so diminutive that one rarely has a good, clear look at them. When a gnatcatcher is seen for the first time, it is strikingly like a scaled-down mockingbird – gray coloration above, white below; long twitchy tail with white borders; slender bill. The two, of course, are not related, but the resemblance is strong. Unlike the mockingbird, however, the gnatcatcher is not zealous to advertise its presence. Were it not for the painfully thin, wheezy *twang* which is its call-note, uttered almost constantly as it feeds, one would rarely be aware of its presence.

There is some disagreement about the family relationships of gnatcatchers. They are among our smallest birds, but totally different from other small bird species. They have been considered members of the Old World warbler family (unrelated to our North American wood warblers), which also includes our kinglets. Some authorities, however, speculate that the gnatcatchers do not belong to this group, that they are actually of New World origin. Whatever their genealogy, they resemble no other birds in our area.

There are eight kinds of gnatcatchers (this is the only one in eastern North America) ranging from southern Canada to the southern parts of South America. This species is found from the most southern areas of Ontario, along lakes Erie and Ontario, across most of the eastern and southern United States. It winters from Florida and California south; I have seen it in winter in the Mexican provinces of Quintana Roo and Yucatan, and in Guatemala. But the birds breed in Mexico as well, so one cannot be sure of the identity of Central American birds at that season.

It is said that the gnatcatcher has a soft, attractive, vireo-like song, but I have never heard it. The characteristic note is the call described above, which never seems to cease as the birds forage for food and work about their nest. In feeding, they are extremely active and fidgety – hovering like hummingbirds, darting out and back again in the manner of a flycatcher, restlessly working among the leaves of deciduous trees.

There is some evidence that insects may be the sole food of this species, barring a few items of vegetable matter under special circumstances, such as those offered at winter feeding trays in the south. But the long and tapered bill is not that of a confirmed fruit or seed eater. The bird's speciality is, as it were, as plain as the beak on its face.

The nest of the gnatcatcher is a delightful jewel, almost as delicate as a hummingbird's. A tiny cup is saddled across a horizontal branch, and the nest, as described by Francis Marion Weston in Bent's *Life Histories*, is "compactly built of plant down and similar materials bound together with insect silk and spider web and covered externally with bits of lichen."

There are four or five incredibly tiny eggs, pale blue-white, dotted brown. When the young emerge, the always frenetic activity of the birds builds to a new pitch of nervous excitement. Urgently flickering about in the leaves, tails flitting, the gnatcatchers resemble nothing so much as little mechanical birds wound tightly to an unbearable degree of explosive energy.

Length 4 inches.   Male, Baton Rouge, Louisiana, November 13.

plate 69—the sketch

CEDAR WAXWING

Bombycilla cedrorum

plate 69 # CEDAR WAXWING *Bombycilla cedrorum*

However one chooses to look at them, waxwings are mysterious and unconventional birds. They are common enough, but their comings and goings, and even their familial ties, are for the most part poorly understood – if they are, in any sense, understood at all. They can be recognized by the uncommonly smooth and silky texture of the body feathering, by the crest and the brightly coloured wax-like droplets on the wing, the function of which is completely unknown. There are three kinds of waxwings in the world, but the cedar waxwing is restricted to North America. The larger and more colourful Bohemian waxwing lives in the northern forests of both America and Eurasia, and there is a third species in Japan.

For the sake of convenience, ornithologists have dumped the waxwings into what Austin calls a "trash-basket" family, along with the four silky flycatchers of Central America (one of which occurs in the United States), the strange palm chat of Hispaniola, and one waif in Asia Minor, the *Hypocolius*. All of these seem to be chiefly fruit-eaters; they live in trees, and they share the soft, attractive plumage. None is renowned for the quality of its voice. Beyond that, their relationship is obscure – if they are related at all.

Except in the breeding season, one is unlikely to see waxwings in the same place more than a day or two in a row. They are confirmed nomads, and seem to oscillate wildly in numbers from year to year. This is a common species, no question, but if one were in the position of having just a day in which to show one to a visiting European birdwatcher, it would be a challenge few of us could meet. These birds are utterly unpredictable, appearing one day to feed upon the fruit appropriate to the season, and disappearing the next.

Waxwings are strong fliers, and they are noticeably gregarious most of the year. They fly swiftly, looking something like starlings in their style, and as they move they give an almost continuous high-pitched, sibilant, lisping call note.

But when they alight, they often seem to disappear altogether. An entire flock may come to rest in the dead topmost spire of a tree, and then remain so perfectly still that if one hadn't seen them land, one could walk right by them.

Cedar waxwings nest unusually late in the season for birds in our latitudes – from midsummer and even later. Don't look for them in thick woods. They prefer partly open country, such as scattered cedar swamps among fields, loose orchards, and situations of that kind. The nest is big, and somewhat unkempt. Young birds are stuffed with insects and berries. Their appetites are enormous. Margaret Nice once reported that food fed to the young may pass through the digestive tract in as little as sixteen minutes. Adults, too, are gorgers. A good hatch of flying insects is snapped up in midair, and, when the mountain ash berries are orange and red, the waxwings never seem to know when they have had enough.

Unlike some birds, these do not seem to be closely tied to their nesting areas, or to the areas of their birth. In one experiment, of seventy-two banded adults only two came back to the same site next year. Of 174 banded young, not one turned up in the same area again. Cedar waxwings raise two broods, usually. They have been seen to begin courtship again, and even to copulate, while the first young are still in the nest. They have even been known to begin laying eggs before the first fledglings had left the nest.

Obviously waxwings are opportunists, nesting and wintering where food supplies are most propitious. Some years, when the pickings have been good for two or three breeding seasons in a row, the populations build up spectacularly. Then, there may be a "crash" in their favoured food, and we sometimes notice great irruptions of waxwings where they may not have been seen for quite some time. The populations have a way of levelling out again fairly soon, and things get back to normal. In winter, though, the birds are never predictable, and no one can anticipate where they will turn up next.

Length 5³/₄ inches. Male, Kershaw County, South Carolina.

plate 70—the sketch

LOGGERHEAD SHRIKE
Lanius ludovicianus

plate 70 LOGGERHEAD SHRIKE *Lanius ludovicianus*

Most of us cherish certain immutable notions about birds (and about a long list of other things, for that matter). When something happens to challenge one of these hitherto unquestioned beliefs, it is worth remembering. Such was my experience with this species one winter day in North Carolina, where the loggerhead shrike is a very common bird.

The North American shrikes are not renowned for their voices, and most accounts of their songs and calls damn with faint praise. However, on the fine January day in question, I happened to be en route to Florida, with my wife and the Henry Barnetts. We stopped to look at some roadside birds, and were immediately struck by a sweet, almost bell-like and ringing note which none of us recognized. We spent some time searching for its source, which turned out to be a shrike; it called repeatedly for several minutes as we watched. It was a wholly unusual and lovely sound, in both quality and tone – sufficiently so to be distinctly remembered after many years. I have never heard it since.

The loggerhead is the only one of the world's seventy-odd shrikes restricted to North America. Its close and very similar relative, the northern shrike, lives in the boreal forests of both hemispheres. Most of the shrikes are in the Old World; there is none in South America. Some of the equatorial African species have extraordinarily beautiful and sometimes complex songs; the family potential is there, it would seem.

It could be said that the shrike is a songbird-turned-predator. The only physical evidence of its proclivity is the specialized beak – heavy, notched, and with a hooked tip – very effective for catching large insects, small birds, and other prey. The shrike does not use its feet for hunting; they are no different from those of any other songbird. When it must carry its prey, it usually does so in its bill. Incidentally, the shrikes have had plenty of time in which to undertake a new way of life and to develop their specialty; shrikes have been around

for the better part of twenty-five million years.

A shrike often looks like a chunky, big-headed mockingbird as it sits immobile on some telephone wire, surveying its hunting domain. But when it flies, it zooms almost straight downward, scuds along close to ground level, then abruptly rises again to alight on the next wire, pole, or shrub. This flight pattern is absolutely characteristic. As the bird flies, one will notice white flashes in the tail and wings, but the latter are much smaller than those of the mockingbird.

This bird is not as large or aggressive as the northern shrike. It follows that birds and mammals play a lesser role in its food requirements. It spends most of its time working on large invertebrates and the occasional very tiny reptile and amphibian, though in winter and at other seasons it is not averse to the lesser birds, and some of the smallest mammals.

The old name for shrike was "butcher bird," not because it eats meat but because of its habit of impaling prey on a thorn or lodging it in the fork of a twig, the better to pull it to pieces. If you are equipped with the bill of a predator and the feet of a songbird, you need some additional purchase for cutting up your food. Sometimes the northern shrike returns to these "caches" in times of lean pickings; the loggerhead is rarely seen to do so. As Sprunt observes in Bent's *Life Histories*, "Food in the loggerhead's range is so abundant and constantly available that there is rarely an occasion when the bird has to resort to already secured prey. Conversely, there are doubtless times when the northern bird is hard put to it in winter and uses a larder far more frequently."

Loggerhead shrikes breed north to the southern limit of the coniferous forest. They are never ones to call undue attention to themselves, and while nesting they are especially self-effacing and inconspicuous. The bulky nest may be in a thick hawthorn or other impenetrable shrub, or in a dense tree. Look for shrikes in rural areas which provide plenty of open space for the bird to search from its lookout perch.

Length 7 inches.   Male, Fort Snelling, Minnesota, March 30.

plate 71—the sketch

WHITE-EYED VIREO

Vireo griseus

plate 71   WHITE-EYED VIREO *Vireo griseus*

GENEALOGIES of some birds are difficult to unravel, and that of the vireos is one of the more troublesome. Their ancestry is thought to lie somewhere between the shrikes and the warblers, but it is by no means certain. Some people believe that vireos are much closer to being shrikes; others even maintain they may have tanager affinities. The confusion probably arises from the fact that all these families of birds are relatively recently evolved, in terms of the geological time scale, and that clear-cut differences between them have not yet become manifest. Since vireos, warblers, blackbirds, and tanagers are all thought to have arisen in the American tropics, it is reasonable to think that at some distant stage they had a common ancestry. There are in the tropics today some birds which seem to overlap family boundaries, and which make the problem all the more vexatious – and fascinating.

There are about forty species of vireos, most of them in the tropics. In North America (north of Mexico) we have twelve; in Canada, eight, of which two are "fringe" species at best. The white-eyed is one of the latter.

No Canadian is going to learn much about the white-eyed vireo by staying at home. This is a bird of the south-eastern United States, which reaches its northern limit in New England and the southernmost parts of the Great Lakes area. It intrudes regularly but sparingly into Canada around Point Pelee, Ontario, but rarely elsewhere. The farther south one goes, the better one comes to know this attractive little bird, especially in the Gulf states, where it lives the year round. It winters as far south as Central America, and is common throughout the greater part of its range.

The smaller vireos – and the white-eyed vireo is one of them – are frequently mistaken for warblers. It will be noticed, however, that a vireo has a much more substantial bill than most warblers, and much less striking colour in its plumage. Vireos run to olive-greens and yellows;

some have wing-bars, but they never show any streaks or spots of any kind. Also, vireos move in a much more sluggish fashion than warblers do. They will do some minor gymnastics, such as hanging upside-down occasionally, but even these tricks are done with a slow deliberation which is characteristic of the family. The white-eyed vireo is more active than most, and as the result it is more likely to be taken for a warbler than the others.

This species can instantly be recognized by its bright yellow sides, its wing bars, and the yellow "spectacles" around its white eye. The eye of the young bird is brown. Even more remarkable than its appearance, however, is its song; once it has been learned, it is rarely forgotten. There are always innumerable ways of attempting to express a bird song in an idiom understandable to people, but this one says something like *chick! widdo-weeo, chick!* with varying additional syllables. No matter what form the song may take, the *chick!* and the *weeo* are fairly standard. One will hear this song coming from virtually every thicket in Florida during the winter, where the white-eyed vireo sings all year.

This is fortunate, for this vireo inhabits the densest tangles, briars, thickets, and thorn bushes. It can be extremely hard to see, but when you hear one singing, have patience. Sooner or later it will come out to have a look at you, and if you do not startle it, it will inspect you at a surprisingly close range.

Like all our vireos, this species eats mostly insects, but in winter in the South it has been known to take food such as "sumac, grapes, and wax myrtle." As might be expected, it nests in the heaviest protective cover available. I have not seen the nest, which Pough describes as "fairly bulky for a vireo, and more cone- than cup-shaped . . . often ragged-looking because of the leaves, moss, wasp paper, and sticks woven in with its soft woody fibres." The bird is a common victim of the cowbird, which shows an uncanny ability to find even the most deftly hidden nests.

Length 5 inches.   Male, Gulfport, Mississippi, March 23.

plate 72—the sketch

YELLOW-THROATED VIREO
Vireo flavifrons

plate 72 YELLOW-THROATED VIREO *Vireo flavifrons*

THOUGH vireos are not distinguished for their striking coloration, the yellow-throated vireo is without doubt handsomest in our area. It is also the easiest to identify, through the combination of white wing-bars and yellow spectacles, throat, and breast. But a glimpse that will afford you those several details simultaneously is rare; this is a bird that likes the high foliage of leafy hardwoods, and it is small and difficult to see. It pays to take your time, and to know its song.

This one sounds something like the red-eyed vireo (always the basic criterion for vireo songs and the one you must learn first), but it sings much more slowly, with longer pauses between phrases, more huskily, and at a lower pitch. To my ear, the quality of the sound is somewhat tanager-like. It drifts downward so slowly and lazily on a warm summer day that you would expect little difficulty in picking out the singer, but he manages to keep himself irritatingly well-hidden.

Yellow-throated vireos are not as common as the white-eyes, but they venture farther north in the Great Lakes region. They like gardens, parks, and farm woodlots where there are plenty of large shade trees, and generally avoid the depths of the forest.

I used to know a very dependable place for yellow-throated vireos just a few miles northwest of Toronto, but that place has been drastically changed, and I no longer have any choice spot at which to listen for these birds with any real expectation of success. They demand the biggest shade trees, and good stands of them, and apparently will not settle for anything less. In parts of its range where Dutch elm disease has had the greatest impact the effect has been clear.

Writing before 1950, Bent observed, "I have always suspected that its disappearance was largely due to the excessive spraying of our shade and orchard trees." Most of our certain knowledge of the effects of pesticides on birds is at the moment confined to some of the larger species such as the bald eagle and the peregrine falcon, each of which is at the apex of a long and often complex food chain. The situation with regard to smaller birds is much less clear, although there now is little doubt that chemical pesticides of many kinds influence every living thing in the environment. In any event, if pesticides have not been a factor in the changing fortunes of the yellow-throated vireo, other environmental changes certainly have. Mature deciduous woodland is its prime need, and there is not as much of that habitat as there once was.

Bent describes the nest as the handsomest of any of the vireos, "even prettier than the best examples of the nests of the blue-headed vireo, and fully as well decorated as the nests of the hummingbird, wood pewee, and blue-gray gnatcatcher, though differing from all these in shape and suspended from the prongs of a forked twig." Like the white-eyed and some other vireos, it is reluctant to leave its nest and is often remarkably tame when approached while sitting. Bent says "it cannot easily be driven from its nest and must often be removed forcibly, sometimes with difficulty," which calls forth in the imagination a picture which I am sure the author did not mean to convey!

For the winter, yellow-throated vireos withdraw to the tropics of their origin, spending the season in Central America, south to Panama.

Length 6 inches.   Male, Asheville, North Carolina, September 10.

plate 73—the sketch

RED-EYED VIREO

Vireo olivaceus

plate 73 ## RED-EYED VIREO *Vireo olivaceus*

ITHOUT doubt, the most impressive way to introduce the red-eyed vireo is to report the famous contribution of Louise de Kiriline Lawrence, who counted 22,197 songs from one bird in the course of a single day! I have sometimes wondered whether that classic record was due more to Mrs. Lawrence's persistence or to the bird's. It is not only the best possible sidelight on the red-eyed vireo, but also a splendid example of ornithological dedication.

The song of the red-eyed vireo is heard in all its persistent continuity almost wherever there are shade trees. Robbins *et al.* call this "the most abundant bird of eastern deciduous forests." Peterson once calculated that it is probably more numerous than the robin. More people know the robin because robins are conspicuous in cities and suburbs, and they are big and to some extent flamboyant. However, it is difficult to picture any area of deciduous trees of any size whatever which does not support several pairs of red-eyed vireos. Listen on any sunny day in June, and be convinced.

The bird sounds rather like a robin, but the song is divided into deliberate phrases, with a pause between every phrase. It tends to go up the scale with one phrase, and to descend again with the next. The bird will sing for many minutes at a time without even appearing to stop for breath. For its indefatigability (or perhaps repetitiveness) it has been nicknamed "preacher" in parts of the South.

This is the largest vireo in our area and by far the most common, and should be your yardstick for identifying the others. The dull colours and sluggish, leisurely movements are characteristic. Notice the relatively heavy bill. You will know the bird not so much by its red eye (young have brown eyes) as by its general olive colour, the bold white stripe over the eye, and the grayish cap on the head. Once you know this vireo, and its song, the others will begin to fall into place.

Like any other vireo, this one is almost entirely insectivorous in spring and summer, methodically working its way along branches and small twigs, incessantly searching for insects, their eggs, larvae, and pupae. In the fall, Pough reports that the birds "relish blueberries, the berries of dogwood, spicebush, sassafras, and magnolia, as well as a great variety of small fruits." They need to stoke up well for their fall migration, which will carry them (flying at night) all the way to South America, from Brazil to Peru.

Although red-eyed vireos forage mostly in the widest canopy of leafy trees, they nest somewhat lower down. Vireos build attractive cup-like nests which are suspended from a suitable crotch or from a fork in a twig. This one is especially handsome, daintily decorated with lichens, bits of leaves, and mosses, and spider webs or similar material. There are three or four eggs. Both sexes are said to incubate, and both feed the young.

This is our most widely distributed vireo, from the Maritimes to the Mackenzie, south to the Gulf Coast.

Length 6¹/₂ inches.   Male, Roseboro, North Carolina, May 2.

plate 74—the sketch

WARBLING VIREO
Vireo gilvus

plate 74 # WARBLING VIREO *Vireo gilvus*

SOMETIMES it would seem as though the vireos as a family had for some reason decided to make a policy of drab inconspicuousness and secretiveness. The most common species – and this is one of them – are surprisingly unfamiliar to most people. But you could never call it a conspiracy of silence. These are among the most vocal of our birds, and by their songs we know them.

Even the most highly coloured of the eastern vireos, the yellow-throated, is something less than brilliant. By comparison, the warbling vireo is very much a nonentity, a plain, gray little bird with a pale eye-stripe and a typical vireo bill.

There is nothing pedestrian about its voice, unique among our vireos. The song of no other species has its warbling quality, which sounds rather like a repetitive purple finch. The songs of most vireos are broken into discernible phrases, but this one is continuous: it spirals upward, ending on a higher pitch than it began. It is like most vireos, however, in its persistence; this species has been estimated to sing as many as four thousand times in a day, during the breeding season. The male is so intent on singing that he will even warble away quietly while he is doing his share of incubating the eggs. Hour after hour, the song continues, usually from a considerable height in the shade trees.

The nest is built in the usual vireo cup-shape, most often fairly high up in a big, leafy tree, frequently placed out near the swaying tip of a drooping branch. When he was living in New Jersey, Audubon watched the construction of a warbling vireo nest just outside his window, and he discovered that in this activity, as in their feeding, vireos can be exasperatingly slow and deliberate. He remarked that as the birds returned from material-gathering forays, "they moved so slowly from one tree to another, that my patience was severely tried." Things moved more quickly thereafter. Audubon reported that the eggs hatched in twelve days, and that the young were on the wing in sixteen days.

I think it is an experience common to most of us to think of a bird not necessarily in the surroundings where we see it most often, but in a special and individual context which for one reason or another made a lasting impression. There is in my memory an especially resolute singer in a small stand of willows on the bank of the St. Lawrence River near Montreal. Not having a vireo's staunch tenacity, I did not count his songs, but do recall that he sang all day long, without perceptible pause, as he made his quiet and leisurely way about, feeding all the while.

Winsor Marrett Tyler's contribution on the (eastern) warbling vireo in Bent's *Life Histories* was published in 1950, several years before the complicated links between synthetic chemical pesticides and birds had been worked out. He sensed, however, that something was wrong. "In recent years the warbling vireo has probably suffered more from the spraying of the shade trees with poison than from the natural enemies that commonly beset small arboreal birds. Their nests have been imperiled by the high-pressure spraying that rocks the elm branches at the vital points of the birds' summer distribution, the roadside trees of our country towns." This was a nice observation; all of us have seen the force generated by the large hoses of the sprayers. Little did we know, however, in 1950, of the insidious residual properties of DDT and its relatives. Perhaps one day we will recognize the total impact of pesticides on insectivorous birds.

Length 4³/₄ inches. Male, Arnett, Oklahoma.

plate 75—the sketch

BLACK-AND-WHITE WARBLER
Mniotilta varia

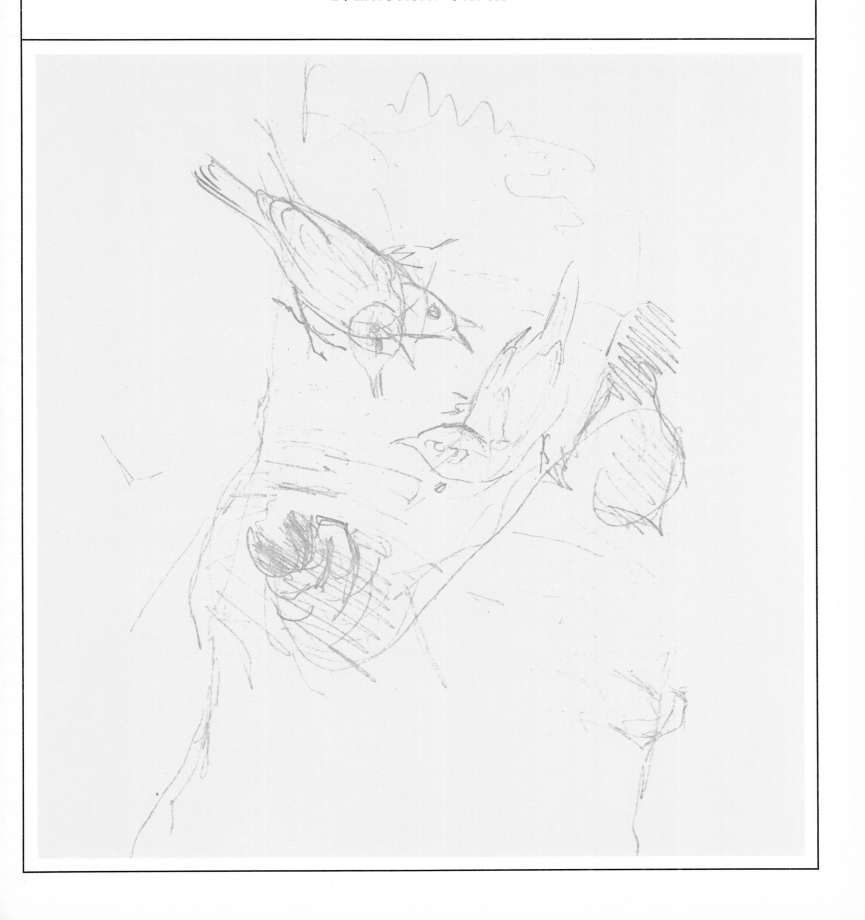

plate 75 # BLACK-AND-WHITE WARBLER *Mniotilta varia*

*A*LTHOUGH this strangely-striped little bird is every bit the true warbler, with its slender bill, its size and shape, and its compulsive hyper-activity, it is marked like no other warbler and behaves like no other. When I was very young I knew it first as the black and white "creeper" (as did Wilson and some of the other early ornithologists, I discovered later). The bird in the hand is clearly recognizable as a warbler, but in the bush its actions are somewhat aberrant.

With the single exception of the similarly-inclined brown creeper, here is the very soul of assiduity and concentration. But where the creeper never varies from its feeding procedure, the warbler, like its kin, is given to improvisation. It works over the trunks and larger limbs of trees with delicacy and precision, flickering from place to place, probing and exploring for insects and other invertebrates. It commonly hangs upside-down, like a nuthatch, or works its way upward like a creeper. At other times it will catch insects in midair with the best of the flycatchers, or perform chickadee-like acrobatics. But generally it sticks to its job of bark-creeping, and it is impossible to confuse with any other warbler in our area.

The only other warbler which looks remotely like this one (and it takes a stretch of the imagination to create any real similarity) is the arrow-headed warbler *Dendroica pharetra* of Jamaica, a rather different, olive-coloured bird which does not creep. I once made an honest effort to turn a black-and-white warbler into the Jamaican species, without success. On June 13, 1968, on the island of Tobago, just a short distance from the Venezuelan mainland, my wife and I saw a warbler which was to all intents and purposes a black-and-white, but which simply could not be – on that date. Despite our efforts to consider the arrow-headed warbler, we had no success. It was clearly an erring black-and-white which had appeared after a heavy thundershower,

and was busily working in its specific fashion on a *Casuarina* – presumably the nearest thing to a northern tamarack it could find. The bird should by that time have been on its breeding territory in the northern United States or Canada, but there it was, a lonely waif undoubtedly lost to its species forever.

This sort of thing happens, of course, and the species is just as well-off without an individual who gets that far out of step. Black-and-white warblers have to know how to migrate and they have to get to the correct destinations. They are among the earliest warblers to arrive in our part of the world, often before the trees are in leaf. This could be a hindrance to those species which depend on insects in opening leaf-buds, but the black-and-white goes straight to work on the coarse bark of the larger trees.

As a rule warbler songs do not match the quality of the birds' plumage; at least they are not especially pleasant to human ears. The voice of this species is typically high-pitched, more remarkable for its upper frequencies than for structure or euphony. The song is wiry and agonizingly thin; it has been described as *wesee, wesee, wesee*, and so on. It is useful to think of the bird as rapidly inhaling and exhaling (which it is not) thus: *ss ss ss ss ss*, like the sound of an elfin saw in wood.

The nest is placed on the ground, and will hold four or five white, brown-spotted eggs. Bent includes a Michigan report from George W. Byers of a black-and-white warbler nest which contained two of the warbler's eggs and *eight* cowbirds' eggs. "His photograph of the eggs suggests that they were probably laid by four different cowbirds."

Black-and-white warblers are fairly common on Florida in winter, but most of them spend the winter in Central and South America as far south as Colombia. They appear to have no hesitation whatever about flying across the Gulf of Mexico, but Sprunt has seen them use the Dry Tortugas as stepping stones.

Length 4³/₄ inches.   Male, Gainesville, Florida, May 10.
Female, Alexandria, Virginia, July 26.

plate 76—the sketch

PROTHONOTARY WARBLER
Protonotaria citrea

plate 76 # PROTHONOTARY WARBLER *Protonotaria citrea*

MANY of the most evocative and historic North American place-names reflect the prevailing attitudes of colonial times so far as wild nature is concerned. There is none of these which I cherish more highly than the Great Dismal Swamp of Virginia and North Carolina. The male bird in the illustration came from there, and it may be difficult for some of us to reconcile the flaming splendour of the prothonotary warbler with all the overtones of dread and mystery which are implicit in the very name of the Great Dismal. As Joseph James Murray pointed out in *The Bird Watcher's America*, "At sun-up in the spring the Great Dismal is vibrant with sounds; at twilight it is truly dismal and any of its strange legends take on credence."

Too many of us think of a swamp as a smelly bog or an impenetrable marsh or some other tangled and muddy situation. A true swamp is a flooded forest with a dense canopy of tall trees (in the south, usually cypress) shading silent, open, fresh water. Too many of us also think only in terms of multitudes of biting insects, squadrons of deadly snakes, and a wide assortment of malevolent, otherworldly beings. Such a place is dark, to be sure, but it is the very gloom that provides the only possible setting for the *nonpareil* among warblers, the golden swamp bird.

"Prothonotary" is a ridiculous name, as all ornithologists have agreed. It means a chief papal notary, who wears a yellow hood. Unfortunately the pompous name was inflicted on the bird a long time ago, and the traditions of nomenclature are stubborn. For the present at least, we – and the undeserving bird – are stuck with it.

It is interesting to consider how many of the world's most brilliant birds live in the almost perpetual shadows of the deepest forests. One thinks of trogons, turacos, so many hummingbirds and cotingas, birds of paradise.

It is as though the intensity of their colouring were somehow too much to be revealed to open sunlight, and had been deliberately reserved for only the most fleeting disclosure. The prothonotary is one of these – an ephemeral flare which burns for an instant in the black mirror of a still pool, and is gone again.

This gorgeous warbler breeds over most of the eastern United States, wherever there are appropriate dark swamps with open water and plenty of drowned and otherwise dead trees for nesting sites. A favourite spot is the stump of a tree, standing in water, ideally containing the old excavation of a downy woodpecker.

This is the only eastern warbler which habitually nests in holes. In one study, Walkinshaw tried bird boxes on the prothonotaries with some success, but found that the birds had competition for tenancy with the much more aggressive house wrens. A small bird's life is difficult: one prothonotary nest in southern Ontario contained no eggs of the rightful owner, but seven of the cowbird.

As is often the case with birds of forests, where the understorey is in dense shadow, the voice of the golden swamp warbler is loud and ringing. It is as distinctive as its colouring – a clear and carrying *sweet, sweet, sweet*, which you will readily recall once you have heard it. The song is quite different from those of the two other warblers with which it might be confused. The blue-winged warbler, which it resembles superficially, lives in a different habitat, and has a black line through the eye together with wing bars. The yellow warbler has yellow wings, and at any distance appears all yellow.

This is a rare and very local bird in Canada. It occurs regularly only along the north shore of Lake Erie, especially at Rondeau Provincial Park, which is somewhat more dependable than Point Pelee. It winters in Central and South America.

Length 4³/₄ inches.   Male, Great Dismal Swamp, Virginia, June 4.
Female, Mount Carmel, Illinois, May 8.

plate 77—the sketch

GOLDEN-WINGED WARBLER
Vermivora chrysoptera

plate 77 GOLDEN-WINGED WARBLER *Vermivora chrysoptera*

At one time or another most of us have inflicted our special interests and enthusiasms on our children. It is possible, however, that we naturalists may be slightly more prone to the habit than some others. It seems that we do so at least until the children are of an age to make a choice, and we hope that we have done the right kind of "conditioning." When my daughter Sally was very small – at that truly magical age when everything is novel and ever so stimulating – I used to take her birdwatching from time to time.

One May morning we happened to find ourselves in the midst of an unusually large warbler "wave." Warblers were everywhere – redstart, magnolia, chestnut-sided, black-throated green, and all the rest. We enjoyed ourselves thoroughly for an hour or two (how pleasurable it is to see old treasures through new eyes), in the delightful process of giving names to new things. On our way home, the little girl stopped, pointed upward, and said, "There's one that's different. We haven't seen it before." I doubted that seriously – six-year-olds see any number of strange and unusual things – but, indulgently, I checked the bird. Of course, it was a fine male golden-wing, its occurrence infrequent enough in our area to be duly noted and filed.

It is always a joy to come across this splendid warbler. Even at the best of times the bird is elusive, and it does not seem to be really common anywhere. The odds against picking many up in spring migration are fairly long, and you need to find a nesting territory in order to be able to venture out with any real expectation of seeing one.

In my somewhat local experience with the golden-winged warbler, it has been a bird of rank, young deciduous growth. Except in migration, you will rarely see it in tall trees, but at that season it often seems to select the very tallest. It may turn up in somewhat dry situations, or in swamps and swales. For nesting, the common denominator appears to be the thickest and densest stands of alder, birch, poplar, and willow saplings. In so far as we have such habitat, it is a "jungle" bird.

When you have an opportunity to observe the golden-wing clearly and at length, you will unfailingly notice its acrobatic behaviour. Like a Nashville warbler, or any chickadee, it does much upside-down feeding. It moves, clings, and flutters from twig to twig with all the grace and dexterity of a kinglet, usually so swiftly that it is not always easy to distinguish its markings.

Essentially, this warbler is gray above, white below, with black face patch and throat. One may or may not see the yellow wing patch clearly. There is wide variation in the golden-wing's song, which is best described as buzzy. Usually the first buzz is followed by others on a lower pitch. The quality is rather different from that of any other warbler except for the blue-wing, and a visual check is always recommended.

Golden-winged warblers breed in the southern parts of the Great Lakes region and New England, and somewhat farther down in Appalachia. In Canada they barely extend through the southern parts of Ontario, but there are records elsewhere. The lower part of the golden-wing's range overlaps with that of the blue-winged warbler, which is so closely related that the two species frequently hybridize. Golden-wings winter in Central America and the northern parts of South America.

Length 4¹/₄ inches.   Male, Gatlinburg, Tennessee, June 13.
Female, Bay St. Louis, Mississippi, September 20.

plate 78—the sketch

BLUE-WINGED WARBLER

Vermivora pinus

plate 78

BLUE-WINGED WARBLER *Vermivora pinus*

IN the experience of bird students in the North, this species is much less familiar than the golden-winged. One very occasionally sees a blue-winged warbler during migration. Farther south, in the east-central States, the bird nests over a reasonably large area, but it is nowhere common, and always difficult to find.

If the bird *is* in the neighbourhood, however, one's search is virtually ended, because it is a persistent singer with a distinctive voice. The first one-buzz note of its song sounds like a golden-winged warbler; this is followed by a peculiar and almost unbirdlike buzzy trill with a strange raspy quality which has always made me think of a miniature "Bronx cheer."

The blue-wing's preferred habitat is somewhat variable, and includes such places as dry, brushy gaps in stands of red cedar, moister edges of alder thickets, pastures grown up with large shrubs – always places with plenty of thick cover. The bird itself is readily identified: the black mark through the eye and the two white wing bars separate it immediately from any other largely yellow warbler.

In those places where the two species occur regularly, blue-wings regularly hybridize with golden-winged warblers. These crosses are fertile, but their appearance is not predictable. The most common form of hybrid, which is known as "Brewster's warbler," looks like a golden-wing with a white face and throat, and sometimes a dash of yellow on the breast. Much rarer is the cross called "Lawrence's warbler," which typically appears to be a blue-wing with a black face patch and throat. I have seen the "Brewster's" several times, "Lawrence's" but once.

Of course there are variants upon the variants, depending upon the (not always apparent) genealogy of the breeding pair. A very strange and mixed assortment of plumages is in the museum collections. The problem has been discussed in detail by Kenneth C. Parkes in the *Wilson Bulletin* (vol. 63, no. 1, March, 1951), and by Ludlow Griscom in *The Warblers of America*. The essence of the phenomenon would seem to be that blue-wing and golden-wing have so recently split away from a common antecedent that both are still having difficulties in establishing themselves as new and distinct species.

A rare event in Canada was the successful nesting at Milton, near Toronto, of a male blue-wing and a female golden-wing in 1956. They produced four hybrid young, and all six birds were taken for the collection of the Royal Ontario Museum. Those who occasionally express regret at the need to "sacrifice" a handful of birds in this way will understand that a clutch of hybrids means very little to the lifetime of the blue-winged and golden-winged warblers as species, but can mean a very great deal to the study of genetics. Such specimens are the raw material of science.

Unlike the active, even acrobatic golden-wing, the blue-winged warbler is somewhat deliberate and slow in its feeding. But it is a strong flier despite its size, spending the winter months in Central America.

Length 4¹/₄ inches.   Male, Milledgeville, Georgia, August 29.
Female, Atlanta, Georgia, September 1.

plate 79—the sketch

PARULA WARBLER

Parula americana

plate 79

PARULA WARBLER *Parula americana*

THE parula warbler is our smallest warbler and also one of the most rewarding: it is common, it is vocal, and it is pretty. Few warblers have such a characteristic song, which is an ascending very rapid trill with a buzzy quality, ending with an explosive *zip!* which is very distinctive. In the south, parula warblers are associated with Spanish "moss" (*Tillandsia*) groves, in the north, *Usnea* lichens.

The word "parula," from *Parus*, means "little chickadee." The bird is indeed very like a chickadee or a titmouse in the way it goes about its foraging. Rather than expending its energies in the constant, hither-and-yon, nervous movements of most warblers, it adheres to the work at hand, clinging, unhurriedly picking and poking. The name suits it, unless one prefers the elaborate and clinically descriptive "blue yellow-backed warbler" preferred by Bent and others. Names of this kind can be dangerous. If we were to adopt a literal approach, we would be forced to call the bird "Spanish moss warbler" in the South, "beard-moss warbler" in the North. It is rarely far away from either.

In the Brownsville area of south Texas, near the mouth of the Rio Grande, there is the Sennett's or olive-backed warbler, which is a tropical version of the parula minus the eye ring and breast band, plus a black mask in the male. This is also a bird of the *Tillandsia*. A third species, the Socorro parula, is confined to the island of that name in the Pacific off the tip of Baja California.

Parula warblers are so steadfastly addicted to their moss (or lichen) that they frequently incorporate the living material directly into the construction of their nest. A kind of cup is fashioned in the midst of the hanging vegetation, which admirably conceals it from all points of view. Often, most careful scrutiny will not reveal it.

Many remarkable observations have been made concerning the parula warbler's tameness in the vicinity of its nest. It will tolerate the closest approach – to the point that the young birds may sometimes be taken up in one's hand. There are even cases (a surprising number of them) where the adults have actually fed young birds which were being held. There are few birds so trusting.

In French Canada this bird is known as *la fauvette parula*; all warblers are *fauvette*. In France the word is reserved for members of the genus *Sylvia*, which includes the familiar European blackcap and the whitethroat. It may be that we have given English colonists an inordinate degree of blame for christening our robin and redstart as they did. The French settlers were homesick too.

In summer in our area, look for parula warblers in spruce woods, or cedar and hemlock groves. They winter in southern Florida, Central America, and the Caribbean.

Length 3³/₄ inches.   Male, Baton Rouge, Louisiana, April 11. Female, Georgia, April 20.

plate 80—the sketch

YELLOW WARBLER
Dendroica petechia

Yellow Warbler

plate 80   # YELLOW WARBLER *Dendroica petechia*

THE fetching little yellow warbler is the most common of its family in our area, the most widespread geographically, and the easiest to recognize. Its vast breeding range extends from Alaska to Labrador and Newfoundland, south to Venezuela and Ecuador. This is our only bird which in the field appears to be all yellow, including the wings. Many rural people know it as "wild canary," or "yellowbird."

Except for the high Arctic, it is almost impossible to go anywhere in North America in summer without encountering a yellow warbler of one sort or another. Seven distinct subspecies, or races, are recognized on this continent, and there are others farther south. Since these races live in so many different kinds of country, it is difficult to generalize about the bird's habitat beyond saying that it seems to like rather small trees or largish shrubs, with plenty of space in between. It all depends where one comes from.

If one grew up in Ontario, and spent much time at Point Pelee, one would be convinced that the yellow warbler is the world's most abundant bird. There, it is most frequently seen in an old apple orchard now grown up with sundry dense vines and tangles and an assortment of young hardwoods, still relatively small. To me, the yellow warbler will always be associated with apple blossoms.

The bird's song is quite distinctive, and a good basis from which to compare and contrast the voices of less familiar species. It is a high-pitched and attractive series of musical notes, thus: *sweet, sweet, sweet, sweet, sweet*, with the last *sweet* higher than the rest. This is usefully differentiated from the louder, single-pitched notes of the prothonotary warbler, for example.

Yellow warblers have the misfortune to be well known for the frequency with which they are victimized by parasitic cowbirds in our part of the world. It should be pointed out, however, that despite the fact that it happens all the time, there does not seem to be any shortage of yellow warblers. These things have a way of working out. Many yellow warblers have actually taken steps to circumvent the cowbird by the admirably direct action of building a new nest on top of the old one, abandoning both cowbird and warbler eggs, and starting all over. As Snyder describes it, "the yellow warbler simply builds another bottom to its nest, literally putting a ceiling on cowbirds' eggs. It may repeat this procedure to the extent that a two or three storey nest results." Bent says the yellow warbler leaves "the alien egg to cool off in the cellar." Multiple nests of this kind with as many as five or even six storeys have been seen. Perhaps we can assume that eventually either warbler or cowbird will tire of the "escalation," and allow the season to proceed.

Any bird so widely distributed and of so many races is clearly a pioneer of sorts. It has even managed to invade such a distant and unlikely place as the equatorial Galapagos Islands. Indeed it may have hit upon the Galapagos more than once, or even several times. There would appear to be two different "kinds" of yellow warblers there now, co-existing at least for the present: one is a brightly-coloured form, the other much duller. Looking at these birds, one begins to wonder whether it might be possible that instead of two races living side by side (which seems rather unlikely), we are actually witnessing the emergence of a new yellow warbler species. The world of birds is really a long list of unanswered questions. It may well be that one day the yellow warblers of Galapagos will draw some of the scientific attention away from the famous finches of the islands.

Length 4 inches.   Male, Covington, Georgia, June 5.

plate 81—the sketch

CERULEAN WARBLER

Dendroica cerulea

plate 81 CERULEAN WARBLER *Dendroica cerulea*

*A*VERY large part of the joy and excitement of birdwatching depends on where one does one's watching. This delicate species provides a case in point. If one lives, say, in central New York or Pennsylvania, in the heart of the big hardwood country, with scattered swamps, the cerulean warbler – delightful though it is – is no novelty. If one lives in Canada, a proper look at the cerulean warbler is rare and noteworthy.

The cerulean was one of the earliest "Carolinian" birds of my experience. I had been warned to expect it at Point Pelee, in southern Ontario. Before my first trip there in the late 1930s, James Baillie of the Royal Ontario Museum had schooled me to the form and quality of its dry, insectlike song – something like a parula, with buzzes on one pitch, the *zip!* at the end being replaced by a longer buzz. Even when so very young and so very much a beginner I had already learned to pay strict attention to anything Billie had to say about the songs of warblers – or any other birds, for that matter.

One unusually warm May morning I remember sitting propped against the base of a small red cedar near the tip of the Point, when the unmistakable series of buzzes I had been taught burst forth immediately over my head. It was unbelievable, but it *was* the cerulean warbler! There it sang, no more than eight or ten feet above me. In those days teen-agers had no access to binoculars, but there was no need for them. I shall never forget that moment, not only for the first sight of a beautiful new bird, but also for the

realization that one *can* depend upon song – even for rarities.

My experience was an exception, so far as the cerulean warbler's normal behaviour is concerned. It usually prefers the highest of treetops and the heaviest foliage. The result is that one will not often manage to see its blue back, because the bird is nearly always directly overhead. All one will see in most cases are the white underparts and the black throat band which may or may not be fully developed. The individual illustrated has a solid bar, but this may very frequently be reduced to a series of spots, some of them joined together.

Since it favours substantial stands of the very largest hardwoods, preferably over swampland, the cerulean warbler is difficult to find in Canada. There is a handful of suitable places in southern Ontario, but they are becoming fewer every year. Virgin stands of Carolinian hardwood are almost extinct in Canada, and most of those that remain are being logged today. Point Pelee and Rondeau parks are the only places where one can reasonably depend on seeing the bird today. I suspect that sixty or seventy years ago the cerulean must have been much more widely distributed than it is now.

But the cerulean warbler is worth looking for. In the right kind of habitat one should listen for its highly individual song (luckily it sings continuously in season), and after much neck-stiffening searching of the tallest crowns of the trees, one may be rewarded. There are brighter, bluer, more readily observable warblers, but the cerulean warbler is special.

Length 4 inches.   Male, Deer Island, Mississippi, April 13.

plate 83—the sketch

PRAIRIE WARBLER

Dendroica discolor

plate 83 PRAIRIE WARBLER *Dendroica discolor*

ALL of us know any number of singularly strange and inappropriate names for birds (Tennessee and Cape May warblers spring to mind, both of which are birds of the boreal forest), but there is none less well-advised than this one. The difficulty is that to change even the colloquial name of a bird requires something more, it seems, than a new decalogue from Sinai. Even then, of course, those of us who have spent a lifetime with one name for one species could never make the change successfully. But in this case an effort would seem worthwhile, if only for the benefit of succeeding generations of birdwatchers.

This is not a bird of the prairies. It is a small, attractive warbler of dry pine and oak scrub and similar brushy areas; in the far south it lives in mangroves. The name is justifiable only in Florida, where the birds are common during the winter, and where there is plenty of both coastal and inland prairie. No other vindication of the bird's name occurs to me, and even that one is tenuous.

But nomenclature is academic, and these things need not bother us so far as the living bird is concerned. This is one of our most interesting warblers because of its strangely rigid habitat requirements, and because its colonies have a way of moving around somewhat unexpectedly over a period of years. The birds may be common in one area for quite some time, then disappear altogether and turn up in a new environment to their taste, almost without warning. Pough, with his unerring ecological sensitivity, suggests that the prairie warbler's "spotty" distribution is because of the "unstable and temporary character of the plant communities it inhabits." It is rather like the rare Kirtland's warbler in its narrow and exceedingly demanding habitat requirements. It likes logged areas after a certain stage of recovery, and old farms which have relatively recently begun to return to a state of nature. Densely-standing tall trees are not its choice.

A bird this intolerant should not be expected to be common throughout its range. In our area the prairie warbler is numerous enough where the situation is exactly right, but it is scarce or completely absent where conditions have changed. It is abundant, however, in south Florida in winter. There is a resident subspecies in that state which lives on the coastal plains in and around the mangroves, and some of our northern birds winter there as well. Often the birds are surprisingly tame. They are also vocal; I have heard prairie warblers singing in south Florida in every month from December to March.

There is no difficulty in remembering the prairie warbler's voice. The song consists of a series of short buzzy trills, each higher in pitch than the last, which gradually ascend the scale. It is immediately recognizable. The bird is olive above, yellow below, with conspicuous black markings on the face and along the sides. You will notice too an obvious "nervous tic": it habitually flirts or tilts its tail – often a most valuable field mark.

Prairie warblers occur in Canada only in Ontario, especially along the piney shores of Georgian Bay. From there, the range extends to about the Mississippi, and south to Florida. Wintering birds reach the West Indies, the Mexican islands, and parts of adjacent Central America.

Length 4 inches.   Male, Greene, Rhode Island, May 15.

plate 84—the sketch

OVENBIRD

Seiurus aurocapillus

plate 84 OVENBIRD *Seiurus aurocapillus*

ALMOST everyone who has walked in spring and summer woodlands has heard the voice of this bird, but relatively few know the source. Indeed when one does glimpse this strange but appealing little bird stepping about on the forest floor, the last thing that would conceivably occur to one is that it might be a warbler, and certainly not that it could be the author of a sound worthy of a creature twice its size.

The bird will be heard long before it is seen. Its strong and ringing call, *teacher, teacher, teacher, teacher, teacher (crescendo* – and then silence), is unmistakable. It is interesting to think how many birds of deep forests have lusty and penetrating voices. Presumably it is more necessary for them, because of the sound-absorbing properties of dense vegetation, than it is for prairie birds, so many of which have light and tinkling voices. This bird, and its relatives the waterthrushes, have the loudest voices of our warblers.

The ovenbird looks more like a thrush than anything else, as do the so-called waterthrushes, the other two *Seiurus* warblers. These three are terrestrial; the others are arboreal. They walk; most of the others hop. The name "ovenbird" derives not from any familial connection (the great South American family of ovenbirds is not represented north of Mexico), but from the odd shape of its nest. I have not seen an old-fashioned Dutch oven, but I know what an ovenbird's nest looks like, and the inference is easy. The nest is built on the ground; its base is not remarkable, but the top is arched or roofed over with materials from the forest floor – grasses, leaves, and bits of ferns; artfully camouflaged. There is a good-sized

entrance (no mere tiny escape-hatch) to one side. The nest is astonishingly difficult to see, even when one knows where it is. I have watched a nest for a period of time, then looked away, only to find that it was impossible to pick it up again until the movements of the bird itself pointed it out once more.

Ovenbirds are frequent recipients of the graceless gift of cowbird eggs. Harry W. Hann, who over thirty years ago conducted a monumental study of the ovenbird *(Wilson Bulletin,* vol. 49 no. 3, 1937), reported that of nests studied by him in Michigan, no less than fifty-two percent contained cowbirds' eggs. It did not however appear to bother the ovenbirds unduly, and the cowbirds were remarkably unsuccessful. Of forty cowbirds' eggs, only ten young actually left the ovenbirds' nests.

Although its common *teacher* call is the best known vocal performance of the ovenbird, it also has a twilight song which is given on the wing. I have not heard this song (or, if I have, I did not attribute it to an ovenbird). It is described by Gross, in Bent's *Life Histories,* as "much more musical and beautiful" than the customary daytime call. Gunn remarks that it is sometimes given at night. "It is also given more frequently towards the end of the breeding season than during the early part of it." It is said that this melodic flight song is occasionally accompanied by a typical *teacher* call, which would leave identification beyond question.

Ovenbirds are common in broad-leaved woodlands east of the Rockies and south almost to the Gulf coast. They winter from south Florida to the northern parts of South America.

Length 5 inches.   Female, Baltimore, Maryland, May 17.

plate 85—the sketch

KENTUCKY WARBLER

Oporornis formosus

plate 85

KENTUCKY WARBLER *Oporornis formosus*

THIS handsome ground-dwelling warbler is not included because either artist or author has had any great personal experience of it – although both of us have watched the bird in the field many times – but rather because it is characteristic of the great hardwood areas of the eastern and central United States. In the moist woods of southern Illinois, for example, there is probably no more commonplace sound than the loud and emphatic songs of this well-favoured species.

Names of birds which carry geographic connotations may often be misleading, as we have commented elsewhere. The Connecticut warbler, for example, inhabits mid-Canada. In the present case, however, the geographical designation is a happy one. Wilson named the bird "for the state in which he found it most abundant," and, as Bent observes, "Kentucky is not far from the centre of its abundance in the breeding season." This was a far happier choice than Wilson's naming of the magnolia warbler, a bird of the northern spruce-fir-larch forest, which he shot out of a magnolia tree while the bird was on migration.

Warblers of the genus *Oporornis* are generally olive and yellow over-all; they generally live near the ground; and they are generally stockier in build and more deliberate in their movements than, say, the more arboreal *Dendroica* species. An adult male Kentucky warbler, with its black mask and yellow spectacles, cannot be mistaken for anything else. Females are duller, but recognizable. Young birds in the autumn are another story altogether however; all immature members of this genus are difficult to recognize at that time of year. Usually there is enough yellow and black around the eye to give you a clue.

The song of this bird is forceful and ringing; it carries a good distance through the forest understorey. Unlike some of its closest relatives, it often chooses a somewhat conspicuous place to perch for singing. I have seen one chanting away from a completely exposed site in a big cottonwood, thirty feet from the ground. Generally, however, the birds are more reclusive than that would indicate. The song is strongly reminiscent of that of the Carolina wren or tufted titmouse – a strongly enunciated *churdle, churdle, churdle* whistled endlessly.

I have never seen the nest of this bird. Sprunt says, "being on the ground, the nest is hard to find, both because it resembles nothing so much as a bunch of leaves, and for the reason that the bird is inclined to sneak away from it on the ground for some distance before flushing." There are said to be four or five brown-spotted white eggs.

Many observers have reported seeing the adult Kentucky warbler perform a "broken-wing act" when its nest was approached. The bird tumbles and flutters about on the ground, giving every appearance of being injured or otherwise in distress. This has the effect, often, of distracting the attention of an approaching predator away from the nest. There is no reason to think that the bird does this with forethought; its "tailspin" is the product of certain inherent impulses when its nest is threatened. (For a fuller discussion of this phenomenon, see the killdeer in Volume I.)

Peripheral in Canada, common in the eastern United States, Kentucky warblers winter from Central America to northern South America.

Length 4¹/₂ inches.   Male, Alexandria, Virginia, April 30.
Female, Baltimore County, Maryland, August 11.

plate 86—the sketch

MOURNING WARBLER

Oporornis philadelphia

plate 86 MOURNING WARBLER *Oporornis philadelphia*

OURNING warblers are essentially Canadian birds in the breeding season; they range from north-central Alberta to the Gulf of St. Lawrence and Newfoundland, south only to the northernmost Great Lakes and New England states. Of course they are seen throughout the eastern United States in the migration seasons.

This is a bird of dense shrubbery and undergrowth, from which the male chooses to emerge to an exposed perch only to declare in song the limits of his territory. The thicker the understorey, the better the bird likes it – around the edges of swales and bogs, on steep ravine slopes, and in overgrown forest clearings.

It is a pity that this species is so elusive, for the male in breeding plumage is strikingly handsome. The adjective "mourning" comes from the black crape-like markings at the lower edge of his gray hood. But let it be known that there is nothing mournful about the bird's song or general behaviour. The only bird in the East with which it can be confused is the Connecticut warbler of north-central Canada, which lacks the crape and has a conspicuous white eye-ring. Where the mourning's range may to some extent overlap in western Alberta with that of its far western opposite number, MacGillivray's warbler, the latter has a broken white eye-ring. One cannot distinguish the young of these two closely-related species; there is no apparent difference between them.

The mourning warbler's staunch affinity for open, second-growth tangles on burned or logged forest country prompts Pough to remark that "it is another of the many birds that have benefited from the bad forestry practices of the past century." (The silver lining appears in the clouds when we least expect it.) There are many birds which have prospered since Europeans arrived: killdeer, mourning dove, and horned lark have all made increasing good use of the semi-deserts we have left in our wake; a host of warblers such as the chestnut-sided and the redstart have taken advantage of changes in forest conditions – most especially in the East.

If this bird is difficult to see most of the time, it is remarkably easy to hear. As with so many ground-favouring, thicket-dwelling birds, its voice is loud and clear. It is also emphatic and "swinging" – a series of notes that sound like *chory, chory, chory, chory*. The male is an absolutely indefatigable singer in spring, which makes the birds much easier to find than would otherwise be the case. Bent reports Wendell Taber's note of a male mourning warbler which sang forty-nine songs in twelve minutes, "the songs being regularly spaced."

Mourning warblers spend the winter in southern Central America and the northern parts of South America. Notice that the male bird figured here (above) was painted from a specimen taken in Colombia on February 15, but it is in good breeding plumage. It would not (had it lived) have arrived at the northern limits of its nesting range in our area until some time about the beginning of June. There is a partial pre-nuptial moult described in the literature as occurring in late February and early March, but this bird appears to have assumed high colour already.

Length 4¹/₂ inches. Male, Rio Viejo, Colombia, February 15.
Female, Fortune Bay, Newfoundland, July 17.

plate 87 — the sketch

YELLOWTHROAT

Geothlypis trichas

plate 87

YELLOWTHROAT *Geothlypis trichas*

With the exception of the ubiquitous yellow warbler, this personable little species, the yellowthroat, is the most widely distributed of its family in North America. There are about a dozen regional subspecies, or races, which are currently recognized. This is the only yellowthroat species north of Mexico, but there are perhaps ten more of various kinds in Central America, the West Indies, and South America.

This bird is quite unlike any other members of its family in our area. It is clearly a warbler, but in its general behaviour it is decidedly wren-like. It cocks its tail, scurries and jitters to and fro, scolds constantly and fiercely, and sings on buzzily fluttering wings. In its nervous excitement and hair-trigger irascibility, it acts much more like a typically volatile wren than one of the active but more generally peaceful and law-abiding warblers.

One will never find a yellowthroat nesting in dense woodland or in dry places. The bird invariably demands water of some kind. Its needs are modest though; sometimes the tiniest wet spot will suffice for a growth of rank vegetation of the size it needs. But the larger the piece of suitable habitat, the better; the edges of wide cattail marshes, the overgrown sides of weedy ponds and lagoons, and all such places teem with these vigourous little birds.

The most immediate evidence of the yellowthroat's presence is usually the male's continuous, rhythmic song. Many interpretations have been offered; the most popular is a repetitive *wichity, wichity, wichity, wichity,* although this is extremely variable from place to place – and even in one place. Gunn emphasizes this in *The Warblers of America:* "Yellowthroat songs in northern and central Ontario seldom adhere to the classic *witchity witchity.* There is much variation and some are scarcely recognizable as Yellowthroat songs. Some are quite complex. Commonly, syllables are added to a phrase and notes in a phrase are repeated." It may be that regional song "dialects" will eventually be as good a clue as any to the race of the singing bird.

Song is constant and energetic through the spring and early summer. The male may sing from the cover of the reeds, or he may climb up a long stalk, hitching up in little jumps, singing as he goes. Sometimes he will fly up out of the marsh in much the style and manner of a long-billed marsh wren, chattering and chittering as he helicopters along like some vibrating insect, then he will drop back into the vegetation, still singing lustily.

The black mask of the male bird is unique; no other North American warbler resembles him. He retains the mask all year round. The female is more difficult to recognize, but notice her yellow throat and plain face, and her relatively large, bright eye. The characteristic movements, and the habitat, both help in identification.

In discussion of the yellow-shafted flicker (Volume I), the significance of sexual identification marks was raised. In the case of the flicker, the male is known by his black "moustache" marks. With the yellowthroat, it is the male's black mask. Peterson has reported on an experiment with yellowthroats conducted by the late great conservationist, William Vogt. He put out a stuffed female yellowthroat, which was duly courted, and copulated with two or three times by a wild male. Vogt then pasted a black mask on the dummy, and the male, in Peterson's words, "returned and was about to resume relations as before when he suddenly noticed the mask. He bounced a full two feet in the air and dashed away as if completely mortified."

Yellowthroats breed in suitable habitat over the entire continent south from the Alaska Panhandle, James Bay, and Newfoundland.

Length 4¼ inches.   Male, Atlanta, Georgia, April 10.
Female, Whitewater Lake, Manitoba, June 6.

plate 89 — the sketch

HOODED WARBLER

Wilsonia citrina

plate 89 # HOODED WARBLER *Wilsonia citrina*

ONE fine spring day shortly after the end of the Second World War, Donald Pace and I repaired to the grassy Toronto waterfront at the entrance to the Canadian National Exhibition grounds to eat our lunchtime sandwiches. It was a welcome relief from the stuffy confines of an industrial building in which we were working up the street. As we lounged on the grass – talking, no doubt, of birds, among other things – a tiny, brilliant yellow-and-black bird appeared on the lawn beside us. Neither of us had ever seen a hooded warbler before, but there was no mistaking it. The bird had absolutely no business being as far north as it was (hooded warblers are stragglers at best in the Toronto region), but it turned out later that a small aberrant "flight" of these elegant birds had appeared that week, soon to disappear again.

It was sufficient surprise to see a hooded warbler in our home region, but an even greater one to see it out in the open, in the middle of a close-cropped lawn the size of a football field. We knew it was a retiring, ground-loving bird of the deep southern woods; it must have been in a sorry predicament to allow itself to be so conspicuous.

In succeeding years, Pace and I became much more familiar with the bird in its proper haunts, which to a Canadian are those swiftly vanishing and infinitely precious stands of southern hardwoods – mostly poorly-drained maple and beech, with rank ground vegetation and plenty of young saplings, filled with the whine of mosquitoes and the flutes of wood thrushes. Hooded warbler country is deep green shade, dappled sunlight, and coolness. In Canada there are few such places – two or three along the north shore of Lake Erie, and a handful of ancient woodlots somewhat inland. For many years Fred Bodsworth, the noted naturalist-novelist who discovered the first Canadian hooded warbler nest, kept a close eye on the birds of the majestic Springwater Woods at Orwell, Ontario. The woods are diminished now; timber "management" is going ahead.

To see hooded warblers where they really belong, you must go to the great and extensive hardwood forests of the United States, east of the Mississippi. There, on lowlands covered by big trees, one can hear on every hand the characteristic ringing song of this lovely bird. The first time I heard it, I knew I had heard something like it before – the voice of the magnolia warbler of the northern forest is similar in form, but not so loud, or strong. There is another way of remembering it, if one does not know the magnolia. In rhythm, if not in pitch, the song repeats the opening notes of the *William Tell* overture, which people of a certain age recall as the theme-music of *The Lone Ranger*. Aretas A. Saunders' interpretation of the song, "*tawit tawit tawit tee too*," may thus be clarified.

The farther south you go, the more numerous the hooded warblers become. I know one spot in southern New Jersey where they are (to a Canadian) extraordinarily common. Bent quotes S. A. Grimes to the effect that in Florida, in the right swampy habitat, "it is usually the most abundant bird throughout the spring and summer. . . . In the swamps most favoured there is commonly a breeding pair every fifty to one hundred yards in any direction."

Like others of the genus *Wilsonia*, hooded warblers stick fairly close to the ground. They are active birds, constantly fanning the tail and revealing its white spots, often catching flying insects in midair. I have never seen the nest, which is described by Pough as "usually between two and three feet up in a fork in a shrub or small tree; made of dead leaves held together with plant fibers and spider webs; neatly lined with grass and fine bark shreds." The birds winter in Central America.

Length 4¹/₂ inches. Male, Essex Co., Virginia, May 5. Female, Christchurch Parish, South Carolina, April 20.

plate 90—the sketch

CANADA WARBLER

Wilsonia canadensis

plate 90

CANADA WARBLER *Wilsonia canadensis*

THE breeding range of this pleasant little warbler extends from central Alberta to Nova Scotia, the northeastern states, and in the Appalachian mountains as far south as Georgia. From experience I tend to think of it chiefly in terms of the St. Lawrence Valley, most especially along the north shore of the river, east of Quebec City, where the dense, undergrown mixed forest is to its perfect satisfaction.

This species is remarkably free of shyness; on its nesting grounds and in migration one can often get surprisingly close to it. There is no mistaking the bird: plain gray upperparts uninterrupted by any white, yellow spectacles and underparts, and the characteristic black necklace. The female illustrated is an autumn bird; even at that season there is a suggestion of delicate dark markings on the breast. No other bird looks like it.

Some years the Canadian warbler is one of the most conspicuous birds in the cooler eastern forests. It likes mature areas, but ones which have a substantial understorey of second growth. Also, it shows a certain liking for water; sometimes it seems that the wetter and danker the surroundings, the better the bird likes it. In *The Bird Watcher's America* Bodsworth has described typical nesting habitat in Ontario's Algonquin Park: "A widespread hardwood forest type in Algonquin today is aspen-white birch because these are the pioneering tree species that produced the first stage of new forest following the fires and lumbering of 50 to 100 years ago." He finds the Canada warblers less numerous in the other deciduous type, "typical of older forest stands that were not burned or leveled during the initial lumbering era . . . a hardwood association with sugar maple and yellow birch the dominant species."

The nest is described by Bent as "on or near the ground, often in a mossy hummock or moss-covered log or stump, or in a cavity in a bank or the upturned roots of a fallen tree." The nest is cruelly difficult to find, however; it always seems to be in the thickest tangles. But the breeding birds themselves are not difficult to discover. Where the area is to their taste they sing loudly and vigorously.

The song is not easily described, chiefly for the reason that it is so variable. It is fast and jumbled, with a mixture of loud *chips* and double *wichy* notes. It generally begins, however, with a loud and distinct *chip*, which is followed by a tumbled welter of notes which, taken together, achieve an attractive warbling effect. No North American wood warbler, however, actually warbles.

Like its closest *Wilsonia* relatives, the Canada warbler is an expert catcher of flying insects on the wing, and appears to take a substantial part of its food in this way. Audubon was so impressed by this that he first called the bird the "cypress swamp flycatcher." In a later plate he identified it as the "Canada flycatcher." When it is not doing aerial gymnastics, the bird actively forages like any other warbler, gleaning insects and their "grubs" from leaves, bark, and other small hiding places. It will not venture far from the ground even for food, and you will almost never see one any distance overhead. On migration stop-overs I have seen Canada warblers searching for insects directly on the ground.

Canada warblers winter a very long way from their breeding grounds – in Ecuador, and in Peru, as far south as Lima. It is said that in this season they move in flocks on both eastern and western sides of the Andes, at altitudes between four and five thousand feet.

Length 4³/₄ inches. Male, Fort Lee, May 20. Female, August 23.

plate 91—the sketch

AMERICAN REDSTART

Setophaga ruticilla

plate 91

AMERICAN REDSTART *Setophaga ruticilla*

THE North American wood warblers have been called, over and over again, the "butterflies of the bird world." The description is most appropriate, and if any one species deserves it more than the others, it must be the charming *candelita,* as the Latin Americans call this scintillating and common bird.

From the Northwest Territories to Newfoundland, wherever there are suitable deciduous woods, and south through most of the United States except for arid regions and the far west, the active, flickering redstart displays its striking pattern and brilliant colour. It constantly fans its tail and wings, almost as though to demand attention. Since it is a bird of mixed second-growth, and since there is so much of that kind of habitat on the continent now, it is probable that redstarts are more common today than they used to be. In spring and early summer, their songs seem to be everywhere in wet woodlands and sapling groves.

Redstarts are unmistakable in any plumage, thanks to the bright patches in wings and tail. These may be flame-coloured, salmon pink, or yellow, depending upon the age and sex of the individual, but they are always present in some form, and the fluttering, butterfly-like motions leave no doubt. This is one species in which young males in their first year may sing, maintain and defend territories, and even breed before they have attained fully adult plumage. These birds look like females, but their flashes are more orange than yellow, and they show more or less sooty black around the face, throat, and wings. It allows one to speculate that (within certain limits) if the bird can deliver the right song for its species, he can attract a mate no matter what he looks like.

The nest is almost always in a young deciduous tree. I have had remarkably consistent luck by concentrating on (for example) birch saplings about two or three inches in diameter whose first crotch may be six or ten feet above the ground. There,

several times, I have found the sitting gray female redstart, as the male poured forth his high-pitched, strangely sibilant song from the surrounding foliage.

Like all our warblers, redstarts are highly migratory, and there are so many of them that you sometimes see astonishing congregations when conditions are right (or, from the birds' point of view, wrong). One memorable morning at Point Pelee in May, a sudden cold snap had sharply reduced the supply of emergent insects. Large numbers of redstarts were moving about on the ground, in the grass, on the sandy beach, assiduously searching for those small invertebrates which might have been warmed up sufficiently to reveal themselves at ground level. They were so busy that you could walk right up to them.

Allan Cruickshank tells of an October migration when fifteen redstarts landed on his fishing boat in the Atlantic twenty miles east of Cocoa Beach, Florida. "They perched on railings, on fishing poles and even on the heads of the startled fishermen!" One should not, however, confuse this sort of thing with "tameness." The Pelee birds, and Cruickshank's, had no alternative, and when the pressure is on a bird, it may behave somewhat unusually. The "tameness" of migrating birds is almost always a sign of exhaustion or hunger.

It is noteworthy that this bird, a warbler, but one that does a lot of flycatching, has developed prominent bristles around the bill like those of the true flycatchers. This is an example of evolutionary convergence: totally unrelated birds who happen to be in the same "line of business" come to superficially resemble one another.

There is one other redstart in North America, the brilliant scarlet, black, and white painted redstart of the southwestern mountains. There are perhaps a dozen more in the American tropics. The true redstart is a small European thrush; this bird, like the robin and the others, got its name from homesick colonists.

*Length 4¹/₂ inches.   Female, Gulfport, Mississippi, July 31.
Male, Alexandria County, Virginia, April 27.*

plate 92—the sketch

BOBOLINK

Dolichonyx oryzivorus

plate 92 ## BOBOLINK *Dolichonyx oryzivorus*

*A*s the horse gradually disappeared from the eastern part of the continent, the population of that imported European street urchin, the house sparrow, partially levelled out. As everyone knows, the birds depended for food to a great extent on undigested grain in the horses' droppings, and also on spilled grain around livery stables and such places. They now seem to have reached a relatively steady population level.

Not so, it seems, with the bobolink, which, if anything, appears to be steadily diminishing in the East. Bobolinks are not city birds, so they are in no way comparable to house sparrows – except that there would appear to be a common relationship to the horse. Bobolinks used to abound in the extensive hayfields which existed to support the horses. The horses are virtually gone; the hayfields are greatly diminished, and so are the bobolinks.

Although bobolinks, since my boyhood, are distinctly less numerous in the area covered by this book, they appear at the same time to have extended their range somewhat westward. They have now reached southern British Columbia, and in the United States they pretty well occupy the entire northern third of the country.

It is interesting that, despite its westward progress in relatively recent times, the bobolink still retains its ancestral migration route in the East. In the autumn, western birds appear to move east, then south, over the Caribbean to South America, where they winter. This would seem to be going out of their way somewhat; western birds should find it much more convenient to fly directly south overland via Central America. But they do not. Bobolink "tradition" is firmly ingrained.

There is a comparable situation with the wheatear, a thrush which has invaded both sides of the Canadian Arctic from Eurasia. Instead of migrating south in this hemisphere as do all the other birds with whom they nested during the summer, the wheatears go back to Europe, then south – all the way to Africa. Presumably they would not find this immense migration necessary if they "knew" that Florida and California were there. A few pioneers are beginning to turn up in the southern states in winter, however. Perhaps a few western bobolinks will begin to take the short cut one of these days. No doubt some already have.

It is the general rule among birds to be darker on the back and paler on the underparts. This arrangement has obvious survival value; the bird is less conspicuous when viewed from above, against the ground, and the same applies when it is seen from below, against the sky. The male bobolink outrageously defies this convention in the spring; he is jet black below and essentially white on the back. He appears to get away with it for the breeding season, but in the fall he reverts to a brown, sparrow-like plumage like that of the female.

All blackbirds are famous to at least some extent for their vigorous and often spectacular courtship displays. The spring flight-song of the bobolink is one of the most pleasing performances in North American nature. The song itself is a jumbled series of liquid notes something like the *plinks* of a small stringed instrument which bubble forth as though uncontrollable – copiously and loudly. As it sings, the bird may take to the air, fluttering on stiffly bowed wings over its field, fairly trembling with agitation and the force of its torrent of musical notes. Or it will sing from an exposed and prominent stalk of grass, raising its feathers to the fullest extent as its song cascades upon the ears of some impressionable female. It is said that even the redoubtable mockingbird cannot reproduce a bobolink's song.

In the South, bobolinks are sometimes known as "rice-birds." In migration they have always been strongly attracted to rice plantations; they like the sprouts in the springtime, and the ripening grain in the fall. At one point in history incredible numbers of birds were slaughtered in defence of the rice. Now, however, the birds are protected legally, and the rice-growing industry in the south has diminished in importance.

Length 6 inches. Male, Laurel, Maryland, May 4.

plate 93—the sketch

EASTERN MEADOWLARK

Sturnella magna

plate 93 EASTERN MEADOWLARK *Sturnella magna*

ESPITE its name, this bird is not a lark. Like the bobolink – and admittedly neither looks the part – the eastern meadowlark is a member of the blackbird family. These are birds of American tropical origin; the large family includes some of our most widely ranging and abundant species, and also some of the most brilliant, including the resplendent orioles, troupials, and many more.

If the meadowlark is not a lark, and does not really look much like the blackbird it is, we can at least point to a strange and very strong resemblance to the European starling. On the ground, as it walks about with its long, pointed beak, short tail, and its waddling gait, it could be taken for a starling. The similarity continues in flight. With its arrow-shaped silhouette, and its habit of alternately flapping and sailing, the bird is remarkably starling-like. At close range, however, it is a different story. The meadowlark is exceptionally handsome and has a voice to match.

The song of the meadowlark is one of the earliest and most pleasant sounds of spring. It consists of a loud, very clear whistle, somewhat "slurred," with good carrying power. Its opposite number, the western meadowlark, is almost identical in appearance but its voice is totally different. The western's even more famous song is a rich, throaty, but musical "gurgle," in no way resembling that of our bird. As Godfrey remarks, "It amazes most people how two species can sound so different and yet look so much alike." Where the two species overlap, as in Wisconsin and Ontario, where you just might see them together, the western may appear to be slightly paler on the back. But do not count on it. You must hear the voice, and, to compound the problem, a bird that *sounds* like one or the other may well turn out to be a hybrid.

We hear the meadowlark's voice so early in the spring because it is a tough and redoubtable bird. It can endure a lot of cold, and goes no farther south in the winter than it absolutely must, and often lingers on windswept and thus relatively snow-free fields as far north as Ontario. But the farther south you go in winter the more meadowlarks one will see. Central Florida is full of them, on fields and roadsides, all winter long. If one looks out a car window, there will be, at almost any point, a brown bird with yellow underparts, a black V-neck, and white tail feathers which it flicks open as it jerkily moves along.

There is a fascinating phenomenon called "evolutionary convergence." This describes a situation in which two completely unrelated kinds of animals living in widely separated parts of the world come to resemble each other (at least superficially) and live in similar habitat. In Africa there is a group of birds called the longclaws, which are members of the family of wagtails and pipits. Some of these have come to bear an astonishing resemblance to our meadowlark; complete with V-neck, brown back, yellow underparts, and white, outer tail feathers. Even the voice is similar; perhaps clear whistled notes are the kind to have if one must compete with prairie breezes. No doubt white tail feathers are good specific recognition marks in the wide open spaces, and the brown and yellow coloration makes sense. But why the black breast mark?

The meadowlark builds a rather elaborate roofed-over nest on the ground. It is frustratingly well-hidden. Usually there are about five white, heavily-spotted eggs. In spring and summer the birds live chiefly on insects (their toll of grasshoppers must be immense), and in winter they concentrate on whatever seeds are left over when most of the other vegetarian birds have long since departed for more abundant pickings in the South.

Length 8¹/₂ inches.   Male, Fairfax County, Virginia, April 12.

plate 94—the sketch

REDWINGED BLACKBIRD

Agelaius phoeniceus

plate 94

REDWINGED BLACKBIRD *Agelaius phoeniceus*

We have heard a great deal in recent years about the blackbird "problem." Several species of blackbirds, including this one, seem to have increased extraordinarily in the last few decades. In many areas, birds such as the redwing have been and are being denounced as "pests." When one thinks about it, of course, a pest is rather like a "weed," which is simply a flower that is not growing in the place one would like it to be growing in. A pest, a weed, a problem, or a nuisance, is a very subjective human declaration – the validity of which is frequently open to critical challenge.

In my childhood, the redwinged blackbird was strictly (or at least essentially) a bird of the marshes. There were plenty of redwings, and in some places their exuberant autumn gatherings represented a nuisance to some people, but not as a general rule. Since that time, however, they have proliferated explosively, to the point where one can find nesting redwings almost anywhere. The marshes no longer seem to be big enough to contain them all. They nest in fields now, and in drier areas, in brushy spots and the edges of woods – even in city parks and ravines.

Why this remarkable build-up? Why redwings? No one knows for certain, but it seems reasonable to think that it may well be related to a super-abundance of suitable (indeed ideal) habitat and food supply in both summer and winter. This is probably especially true of the winter, when wide stretches of standing crops in the South allow a much higher rate of redwing survival than used to be the case. The historic attrition of winter-kill may have been substantially reduced, allowing more birds to return to their nesting grounds and to breed successfully next spring. Here there may be a "pre-adaptation" involved. The redwing need not have originally evolved as a marsh bird at all – most of the blackbirds are arboreal – and so as their traditional nesting sites became over-crowded the adaptable birds simply moved into situations for which they had been perfectly well-suited all along.

A good example of the new-found blackbird bonanza is in southern Ontario, where mile after mile of uninterrupted cornfields offer an open invitation to immense flocks of blackbirds in the autumn. They stream out of the nearby marshes by the thousands and descend upon the corn like clouds of locusts. The corn growers react, and complain, and official steps are taken – sometimes drastic ones, sometimes humane ones, such as simple scaring devices.

The point of all this is that single-cropping is a grievous insult to nature. Nature responds accordingly. The only healthy ecological community is one that is sufficiently diversified to allow the operation of natural checks and balances to the end that no one species of plant or animal is permitted to reach "pest" proportions. Huge acreages of one crop – whether it be corn, rice, wheat, or whatever, encourage fast-breeding animals to increase beyond the ability of the natural community to sustain them. As a result, the animals resort to the unnatural food supply so bountifully provided for them.

There is no finer sight in our part of the world than the early spring flight of the redwings. A few aimlessly drifting birds seem to arrive first, and then there comes the huge flight of spring males. (The birds tend to segregate themselves by sex during the winter when you will see very large flocks mostly of one sex or the other.) Males set up their nesting territories upon arrival, announcing and identifying them with rollicking songs and vivid display. As the female flocks arrive, the males try to gather as many mates as possible into their territories; they are commonly polygamous.

The redwinged blackbird is colonial to the extent that the territories are quite small, and they adjoin each other closely. There may be several nests in one male's area. He will also build, after the fashion of some wrens, dummy nests which may be pressed into service as he attracts additional hens.

The prevalence of redwings, though a nuisance to some agricultural people, does not seem to have had any deleterious effect on other native birdlife with the possible exception of the bobolink. The verdict on that is still "not proven."

*Length 7¹/₄ inches.   Male, Cranberry Glades, West Virginia, June 16.
Female, Slovac, Arkansas, April 2.*

plate 95—the sketch

ORCHARD ORIOLE

Icterus spurius

plate 95 ORCHARD ORIOLE *Icterus spurius*

THE common name of this bird is more apt than many; it is indeed to be associated with orchards. The scientific name, on the other hand, has an interesting background. At one time there was some confusion between this species and the Baltimore oriole, the female of which was confused with the male orchard oriole – hence, a "spurious" Baltimore. However, that is all straightened out now, although female and sub-adult male plumages of both species sometimes cause confusion for the inexperienced bird watcher.

Most of the eastern United States is home for this uncommonly attractive bird, but it is very local in Canada, occurring only in a slim ribbon of extreme southern Ontario, with a solitary outpost in Manitoba. It is not really common anywhere, however, and if one wants to see it in any numbers, one should go to Point Pelee in the spring. That is the only place I know where one can depend on seeing plenty of these immaculate blackbirds, and hear their pleasant songs in profusion. To my ear, the orchard oriole is somewhat reminiscent of the fox sparrow; for some, the robin is brought to mind. There are references to the bird's singing in flight, which I have not observed.

Like the much more common Baltimore oriole, this species has no hesitation about taking up residence around human habitations. Orchards are their special delight, as are quiet rural areas with plenty of shade trees. They appear to especially like trees which overhang roadways. Where the birds occur in numbers, they are willing to nest at much closer quarters with each other than any Baltimore oriole would tolerate.

The adult male in spring is unmistakable in his impeccable black and seal-brown plumage. First year males are more difficult; they are chiefly olive-green but they have a black throat. They will sing, and breed, in this plumage. Females are greenish-drab; unlike the hen Baltimores they show no hint of orange. Autumn comes early for these tropic-oriented birds; they leave us by midsummer, at which time the young birds look very like the females. During the winter the adult male's colours are still recognizable, though much muted. At that season I have seen orchard orioles in southern Mexico and Guatemala, although they retreat as far south as Colombia.

Bird study is full of imponderables and inexplicables but there are few ornithological phenomena so tantalizing as the strange activity indulged in by many birds, known as "anting." For reasons which are still far from being clear, a bird will upon occasion crouch down on an ant hill, pick up ants in its bill, and busily rub them through all parts of its plumage, almost as though it were dressing its feathers. L. M. Whitaker reported in *The Wilson Bulletin* (Vol. 69, no. 3, 1957) on a captive orchard oriole which would go through this puzzling performance for as much as three-quarters of an hour at a time. A total of 148 species of birds have been known to "ant."

In the absence of a better explanation, some of the earlier observers concluded that the bird so engaged was storing ants away in its plumage for convenient transport to some other place where they could be eaten at leisure, or for delivery to its young. This is not as fantastic as it sounds; certain parakeets are known to carry nesting material by lodging it in their feathers. But it does not seem to be the answer to "anting."

It is known that worker ants contain formic acid, and it may be that formic acid is useful or desirable for the maintenance of a bird's feathers. It is known that formic acid has some properties as an insecticide, so perhaps it discourages parasites. I think it not completely beyond possibility that the bird may also enjoy the tickling sensations so produced; all mammals like to be scratched – so why not birds? When ants are not available, however, birds have been known to use some bizarre substitutes. Welty lists "beetles, bugs, wasps, orange peel, raw onion, hot chocolate, vinegar, hair tonic, cigarette butts, burning matches, and smoke."

Length 6 inches. Female, Canal Zone, Panama, February 28. Male, Whitmore, South Carolina, June 4. Sub-adult male, Fort Snelling, Minnesota, June 3.

plate 96—the sketch

BALTIMORE ORIOLE
Icterus galbula

plate 96 # BALTIMORE ORIOLE *Icterus galbula*

THE word "oriole" is the result of another one of those historic misunderstandings which have confused and bedevilled bird watchers for many years. The true orioles are Old World birds, none of which is represented in this hemisphere. Our orioles are members of the American blackbird family; they are more properly called troupials. Many of these birds are brilliantly coloured; the American tropics abound with them. We have in our area, however, only two that we call "oriole" – the natty black-and-brown orchard oriole, and this one, which wears the orange and black colours of the colonizing Calvert family, the Barons Baltimore, whose territorial grant north of the Potomac eventually became Maryland.

We are singularly fortunate that so many of our most ornamental birds are so common in cities, gardens, and parks. On a sunny spring day, if one were actually to count the individual sources of the whistled notes of orioles from city elms, one might be surprised at how many there are. During the height of the nesting season, city streets and town squares, country lanes, and open woodlands are filled with the rich songs of these blazingly colourful tropic invaders. Elm trees are always especially favoured, but in their absence almost any broad-spreading shade tree may be used.

For all their dedication to song, the birds are singularly difficult to see, as they forage somewhat sluggishly and inconspicuously in the heart of the green canopy. At the height of courtship proceedings, one may glimpse a fiery dart streaking from tree to tree, or perhaps two of them as the males chase each other from breeding territories or pursue the somewhat duller-coloured females of their choice.

Many of our American blackbirds are distinguished for their artistry in nest-building – among them the troupials, caciques, oropendolas, and the orioles. Some of the swinging, pendant nests of the colonial oropendolas may dangle for as much as six feet. The nest of the Baltimore oriole is more modest in size, but it is a masterpiece of delicate weaving. In Bent's *Life Histories*, Winsor Marrett Tyler described this species as "perhaps the most skilful artisan of any North American bird."

The hanging nest, which is ingeniously fastened to a twig crotch toward the tip of a drooping elm branch perhaps thirty feet or more from the ground, is a delicately-woven, purselike structure. It hangs six inches or more from its branch and has an opening at the top. These nests are strong; they are whipped about cruelly in some summer storms. They are not easy to see; in the midst of dense summer foliage they are very inconspicuous. When the leaves fall in autumn, however, they are so very apparent that you wonder how you could have possibly missed them during the season.

For their weaving, the orioles use any suitably long, slender and pliable plant material or other string-like substance. Usually it consists of delicate fibres, but twine is often used, and in the horse-and-buggy days horsehair was common. The cavity is lined with finer material. Despite their strength and durability, the nests are rarely used in another breeding season. The number of blackened old nests you will see along a street or country lane does not in fact reflect the abundance of the Baltimore orioles in any given year.

Pendant nests are common in all the tropics of the world. No doubt they evolved as a means of foiling arboreal predators of various kinds. But predators evolve, too, and in equatorial regions there are many sorts of slender and agile tree snakes quite capable of entering a hangnest no matter how skilfully it is constructed.

The Baltimore oriole summers over the greater part of eastern North America east of the Rockies, north to the limit of broad-leaved trees. It winters in Central and South America. Bullock's oriole, its counterpart in the West, has an orange face and much more white in the wing.

Length 6¹/₂ inches.   Male, Panama, February 26.
Female, Costa Rica, April 8.

plate 97—the sketch

COMMON GRACKLE

Quiscalus quiscula

plate 97   COMMON GRACKLE *Quiscalus quiscula*

*I*ɴ the latitude where I live, the third week of March is often blustery, cold, and unpleasant. It does have its very occasional springlike days, but not many of them. Year in year out, however, the period between the middle and the end of March is enlivened by the arrival of the first male grackles – rude, noisy, arrogant, and utterly captivating in their roguishness. Big, sturdy fowl (they use to call them crow blackbirds), the grackles announce their presence loudly and obstreperously. There is no missing them. They make their occupation of a garden evident immediately, with strident, creaking voices; they march stolidly across lawns that may or may not be free of snow. They will roost for a while in sheltering evergreens, then move steadily northward again through the gales. Flocks of females will follow somewhat later.

Grackles are extremely abundant birds in North America, especially in farming areas, where they like to nest in loose colonies in the rows of Norway spruces that were so widely planted in earlier days. At non-breeding times they gather in incredible numbers. One count at a favourite wintering site in Georgia revealed over two million birds. It is anyone's guess how many grackles there are on this continent, but there is scarcely a farmyard or city park east of the Rockies and south of the boreal forest that does not have a high density of these uproarious rowdies.

The authorities used to recognize two distinct species of common grackles – the "purple" grackle of the Southeast and the "bronzed" of inland areas and the North. The two have now been joined under the collective name; they remain only as subspecies. There is no disputing the difference in their colour; these are races that *are* identifiable in the field by the average bird watcher. Both are illustrated here. The top one is a southern individual from Georgia, a typically purple bird.

These usually have bars of iridescence on the back. The lower one, the only form which occurs in Canada, is clearly bronzy, with no bars on its back. Both are males. Head colour is extremely variable, and is not a good subspecific mark. Females are smaller and not so brilliantly coloured, although the intensity of colouring varies with the individual. In the deep South, including Florida, there is a smaller purple form.

Apart from its size (the grackle is much larger than any other blackbird in our area), this bird is recognizable by its especially long tail which, in the male, is folded in a way that makes it resemble the keel of a boat. This is particularly noticeable when the bird is in flight.

Grackles will discover and eat almost anything, and their feeding habits are as diverse as their food items. They will poke their long bills into a lawn in search of "white grubs;" they will carefully explore hedges and shrubs for the nests (and eggs and young) of smaller birds; they will linger around garbage cans and dumps for whatever tidbits may come along; they will follow plows in order to pick up worms, beetles, and other invertebrates; they will patrol beaches for flotsam; they will even eat acorns.

Their manner of dealing with acorns is interesting. Where a jay will hold an acorn in its feet and break it with blows of its beak, a grackle will take an acorn in its bill and simply crack it, with great pressure. This feat is apparently accomplished by means of a "palatal keel" in the roof of the mouth, which holds the acorn steady. The grackle has a lot of accomplishment going for it. In its general food habits it is rather more like a crow than the other blackbirds, and all share a deep fondness of grain in season. The bird's resourcefulness and high adaptability have resulted in the species' spectacular success in the face of human settlement.

190   *Length 12 inches.   Male, Georgia, March 4.*
Male, Tompkins, Newfoundland, May 6.

plate 98—the sketch

BROWN-HEADED COWBIRD

Molothrus ater

plate 98 ## BROWN-HEADED COWBIRD *Molothrus ater*

THE North American blackbirds are a varied and diverse lot, but none is stranger than the cowbird. Its name derives from the fact that small flocks habitually associate with domestic cattle in fields (in the old days they called it "buffalo bird"). I have seen one perched on the back of a moose. It would seem that the birds avail themselves of small insects stirred up out of the grass by their larger companions, in much the same way that African cattle egrets benefit by walking about between the legs of elephants and buffalo.

Its partiality for the company of larger creatures is by no means the most remarkable thing about the cowbird. Like the well-known European cuckoo, it customarily lays its eggs in the nests of other birds, leaving the foster parents to raise the young cowbirds. Nest parasitism in a family of birds which includes such renowned weavers as oropendolas and orioles seems a strange anomaly. But there is nothing ordinary about any blackbird.

Cowbirds appear to be of South American origin. There are eight species all told, four of which are known to be parasitic. But the habit is not restricted to those birds and the European cuckoo. Ducks of several species are known to lay at least occasionally in the nests of other ducks, and so are some rails. There are records of American cuckoos doing the same. The honey-guides of the Old World tropics have developed an especially heinous technique: the young honey-guide hatches out of its egg equipped with a fearsome hook on its bill, with which it forthwith does in the rightful nestlings, thus taking over sole occupancy so there is no competition for food brought by the foster parents. Its infamous deed accomplished, the young honey-guide then loses the hook on its bill and becomes a perfectly ordinary and innocent-looking baby bird.

The young cowbird does not kill or evict its nest mates in anything resembling the style of a honey-guide (although a female cowbird will on occasion remove the owner's egg before depositing her own). In general, the cowbird nestling is much larger and stronger than its nest mates, which are usually birds the size of warblers or sparrows, and in the ten days or so of its nest life it undoubtedly has some effect on the other birds through crowding. Cowbirds are known to have parasitized some two hundred and fifty different species of birds.

Scientists have wracked their imaginations in attempts to understand how the parasitic habit evolved in the first place. It has been suggested that the birds had to do it in order to keep up with the nomadic bison. This hardly seems likely; certainly there is no evidence upon which to base it. Another thought has been that a female bird "caught short" and unable to retain her egg simply dropped it in the first available nest, and the habit became part of the normal cycle of the species. This seems unlikely also, in view of the fact that many birds at least occasionally drop eggs away from the nest, and they have not developed the parasitic habit.

Better explanations have been put forward by Francis Herrick, the famous authority on the bald eagle, and Herbert Friedman, who has studied the cowbird exhaustively. It is suggested that the habit originated not on the Great Plains but in the tropics, where the birds evolved. In some way the birds may have lost the delicate synchronization between inherited urges to build nests and to lay. If these got turned around somehow, so that courtship, mating, and laying preceded the nest-building drive, then parasitism could result.

When I was a boy I was always at pains to remove a cowbird's egg (white, speckled with brown, usually larger than the host's) if I came across one in the nest of a little chipping sparrow, yellow warbler, or some other. But later reflection has indicated that there is a healthy balance here; there would seem to be many more host birds than there are cowbirds, and absolutely no sign whatever of undesirable effects on the species victimized.

Next spring, watch cowbirds more closely. Notice especially their mating displays. There are few birds in our area which are so rewarding.

*Length 6¹/₂ inches.   Male, Virginia, March 4.
Female, Baton Rouge, Louisiana, January 20.*

plate 100—the sketch

CARDINAL
Richmondena cardinalis

plate 100   # CARDINAL *Richmondena cardinalis*

BIRD zealots become all too accustomed to a
full measure of grief – the decimation of
seabird populations by oil pollution of the
sea, for example, or pesticidal obliteration
of birds of prey, loss of habitat for the ivory-billed
woodpecker, over-shooting of game fowl, and
so on. So when a genuine success story comes
along – especially one involving a bird so striking as
the cardinal – it is eminently noteworthy.

Prior to this century the cardinal was unknown
as a breeding bird in Canada, and in the United
States it was regarded as strictly a "Carolinian"
species. In the intervening years it has expanded
its range remarkably: Snyder calculated at least
250 miles northward in one thirty-year period.
The cardinal first nested in Toronto the year before
I was born; in less than fifty years it has become
one of our more familiar garden birds, and
now has moved as far north as the edge of the
Laurentian Shield. Cardinals now turn up at least
occasionally around Montreal and as far north
as southern Saskatchewan.

There are those who have said that this reflects
a warming trend in our climate. Climatic change
is a very slow process, and it is difficult to relate the
rapidity of the cardinal's range expansion to that.
In Toronto, for example, where records have been
kept since 1840, it has been calculated that the
historic increase in temperature has been about 3 °F.
a century, not marked enough to account for the
bird's having taken advantage of it to the extent
that it has.

The reason for the cardinal's advance would
appear to be the widespread availability of optimum
habitat. This is not a bird of the deep forest. In
earlier times no doubt the extensive stands of
original woodlands kept it hemmed in to the south.
Then, as clearing took place on such a vast scale,
as farmlands became overgrown with tangled
shrubbery, and as city parks and ravines became
available, the cardinals took advantage of this
situation. It seems to have taken the birds longer
to make the jump in the East because of the wooded
nature of so much of New England. The northward
movement probably took place by way of Ohio,
where conditions were more suitable, then
over into southwestern Ontario (the first Canadian
nest was at Point Pelee in 1901), thence eastward
and northward. It may well be that in due
course those areas of New England not yet
occupied by cardinals will receive their first birds
from the eastward-moving Canadian population
rather than from the south.

Cardinals are sedentary: they do not migrate.
Their northward pioneering is all the more
noteworthy for this. We can picture birds taking
their chances during the nesting season, then
withdrawing quickly at the onset of a northern
winter, but where the cardinal breeds, there it stays
the year round.

A cardinal was involved in one of the most
curious observations of bird behaviour ever
recorded. We all know that birds obey certain
innate impulses or drives at various times of the
year. The drive to migrate, the drive to indulge in
territoriality and courtship, the drive to nest, to
feed young, and so on. The last impulse led
one female far beyond the limits of biological need.
For several days, this bird fed worms to *goldfish*
in a small ornamental pond! The fish would come
to the edge of the pool, open their mouths, and
the bird would pop in the worms. Welty suggests
that "it seems likely that the cardinal, bereft of
its young, approached the pool to drink, and was
met by gaping goldfish accustomed to being
fed by humans. The two instinctive appetites, one
to feed, the other to be fed, magnetically attracted
each other, and a temporary, satisfying bond
was set up." A photograph of this otherwise
incredible event, by Paul Lemmons of Shelby,
North Carolina, appears in Welty's *The Life
of Birds*.

One of the earliest cardinal nests in my
recollection was also the strangest. It was in the
very middle of the city, where a florist's shop
maintained a large greenhouse. A broken pane of
glass allowed the birds access to the warm and
green interior, where they built a nest and raised a
brood of young. The secret of the cardinal's
success is adaptability.

*Length 7³/₄ inches.   Female, Athens, Georgia, February 14.
Male, Houma, Louisiana, May 10.*

plate 101—the sketch

ROSE-BREASTED GROSBEAK

Pheucticus ludovicianus

plate 101 ## ROSE-BREASTED GROSBEAK *Pheucticus ludovicianus*

THERE are certain birds which have an indefinable quality about them. No matter how familiar one may have become with them, they never fail to evoke special enthusiasm and delight. The splendid rose-breast is one of them. It is by no means an uncommon bird – there are plenty of them in our hardwood forests – but they have a kind of magic about them that many of their closest relatives and other even more beautiful species for some reason lack.

This robust finch is an aggregation of contrasts – the male is so resplendent, the female so prosaic. At times the grosbeak is frustratingly difficult to see; at others, especially in migration, it is almost ludicrously approachable. The voice of the bird in full song is so gracious, lilting, and melodious, but its wretched little call note would scarcely do credit to a hummingbird.

Birds are supposed to be well-camouflaged, for perfectly practical reasons of survival. Yet in this species the conspicuous male does his share of incubating and brooding, and even dares to sing while he is at it. This is an arboreal bird, nesting in shade trees, yet at times it will feed on the ground. It is a finch, yet in some of its attitudes and movements it acts like some sort of small parrot. It is extremely migratory, successfully making a voyage which at its greatest extent is between points as distant as northwestern Canada and Ecuador, yet it often seems strangely awkard and inept in flight when one comes upon it in the woods. The sum of its parts is much more than just one more finch.

I have a childhood memory of an ancient and faded rose-breasted grosbeak mounted and gathering dust in an old glass case at school. One day a teacher showed this bird to the class and announced to my utter astonishment that this was a relatively common nesting species right there in our city. I simply could not believe it; although the specimen was by no means bright, all the potential was there. When spring came around, it was time to try to find one. It developed that the search did not take long at all. The grosbeaks, travelling in their somewhat languid bands, often in company with scarlet tanagers, were surprisingly evident. Once one had been taught the thin *pink!* which is the call note, the rest was relatively easy. In life, of course, the male turned out to be infinitely more sensational than any specimen or portrait. As he moves, the bird seems to become more striking every instant, with his rosy wing linings (obscured at rest), and the eye-catching black and white pattern of wings, back, and tail as he flutters away from you.

Rose-breasts will sit tightly, and it is remarkable how easily one can miss a male bird or even a small group of them; they sit stolidly and unmoving as one passes. Obviously the hens are even more difficult; they look like overgrown stalwart house sparrows, but on closer inspection they have a subtle, gentle beauty of their own. The female of the black-headed grosbeak, this bird's opposite number in the West, is very similar but more orange. The males are completely different, but due to the similarity of the females, it is no surprise that the birds occasionally hybridize where their ranges overlap. To me, their voices are indistinguishable.

We are fortunate in our grosbeaks. In the winter we have occasional and unheralded visits from the attractive but unassuming pine grosbeaks, and more regular invasions by the aggressive and obstreperous flocks of evening grosbeaks. The gorgeous cardinal sings all year round. But for a few brief weeks in summer we enjoy the loveliest of them all. The apt but unappealing popular name of the rose-breast, "potato bug bird," sheds more light on its food habits than on its form and nature.

Length 7¼ inches.   Male, Cook County, Illinois, May 9. Female, North Carolina, June 22.

plate 102—the sketch

INDIGO BUNTING

Passerina cyanea

plate 102 # INDIGO BUNTING *Passerina cyanea*

UNFORTUNATELY some of our most intensely blue birds are a great deal less colourful in actuality than they appear to be in illustrations and museums. It is a question of light. One must have perfect light conditions for the appearance of the blue, a mechanical effect of light refraction.

The indigo bunting is a small bird, and it likes to sing from a high perch. The most one usually sees of it (despite its great numbers) is a little black silhouette against the sky. On those uncommon occasions when one can contrive to manoeuvre the bird into full sunlight, below eye level, the brilliance thus revealed is almost unbelievable.

A fully adult male indigo bunting is our only all-blue bird. First-year males are usually not all blue, however, and this frequently leads to reports of blue grosbeaks in areas where blue grosbeaks have no business being observed. It is a southern bird, rarely venturing as far north as our area. It is much larger than a bunting, and the blue male shows two conspicuous brown wing bars. The difficulty is that so many young male indigo buntings also show more or less brown in their wings.

Indigo buntings have several distinct plumages, but since most of the illustrations in the guide books were painted from immaculate adults, we are not always completely aware of them all. In spring migration a fully blue male bunting is the exception rather than the rule. Indeed, some of the birds may well still be in the process of completing their prenuptial molt while they are moving northward. (The males turn brown in winter, with bits of blue in the wings and tail.) There are sundry dappled, in-between plumages.

There are a lot of indigo buntings. Our city parks, ravines, and tree'd suburbs are filled with them – wherever there are good-sized trees with plenty of ground cover and thickets for nesting. A rather drastic but very illuminating experiment by Griscom points out how many birds there are – including surplus individuals ready to move into someone else's vacated territory. Griscom removed the male of one pair; the female had found a new mate by the next day. He removed that male also, and continued to similarly treat each successive male until he had taken nine. The tenth he left to "help raise the family." This is an excellent example of the way nature provides for and anticipates population disasters; there is always an inventory of "unemployed" birds ready to take over.

The indigo bunting is an indefatigable singer, and the song has volume and character. It consists of a rapid succession of notes, in which strongly accented phrases are often repeated, but so swiftly that a jumbled effect is the result. The opening phrases are the loudest, and the song tends to trail off at the end. But no matter. In a few seconds the bird will sing again, often from the dead tip of a shade tree, or from a telephone wire. Borror states that he has no record of any two birds singing exactly the same pattern. This variability is part of the song's charm. The characteristic style of phrasing and a somewhat "brassy" quality make the song quite distinctive from that of the somewhat similar goldfinch. As Tyler says, the bird "throws the notes out for all he is worth."

These charming little birds breed over almost the entire eastern half of the United States, coming into Canada only in southern Manitoba and the Great Lakes region and southern Quebec. They winter in the West Indies and Central America. At least one individual bird migrated so successfully and accurately that two years running it was found in the "same jungle clearing" in Guatemala.

Length 4¹/₂ inches.   Male, Sugar Creek Prairie, Richland County, Illinois, June 2. Female, Arnoldsburg, West Virginia, May 23.

plate 103—the sketch

AMERICAN GOLDFINCH

Spinus tristis

plate 103 AMERICAN GOLDFINCH *Spinus tristis*

Though very few of our songbirds are gregarious at all times of the year, the little goldfinch is the acme of amiable sociability. You will scarcely ever see a solitary individual. Even in the nesting season goldfinches are remarkably easy about territorial prerogatives, although males will pursue males, and females will chase females. The accessibility of food and the company of their kind seem to outweigh other considerations. In the non-breeding season, flocks often number hundreds of birds.

This is the familiar "wild canary" (not to be confused with the yellow warbler) of open farmlands. Small flocks of steeply undulating, softly twittering yellow birds are characteristic over open country with scattered trees and brush. The true canary is an Old World serin of the Canary Islands, but this is the nearest thing we have to it on this continent.

Goldfinches are notoriously late nesters. It seems that they must await not only the ripening of the seeds they require for their young but also of some of the plant materials they use for nest-building. Always sociable, the birds pair before they begin to build the nest, and good-sized flocks are well known even in midsummer, long after most other birds have gotten their broods well-advanced, or even on the wing.

Shaped like a cup, the nest is an attractive and delicate structure made of mosses and bits of grass, with the inner portion exquisitely lined with thistledown. It is reported that the nest is so well woven together that it will actually hold water, and that in times of severe rain, young birds have even been drowned. The fact that the birds must wait until the season is sufficiently advanced that suitable plant materials are available is illustrated by the fact that it takes them about twice as long to build a nest in July as it does in August, when the thistles, milkweed, dandelions and others are at their best. The nest height is variable, but it is generally within a few feet of the ground. The birds have been known to dismantle the old nests of yellow warblers, Baltimore orioles, and others, and to use the materials for their own nests.

The female appears to do all the nest building and incubation. She sits remarkably closely, rarely leaving the nest, and perforce she must be fed. The male comes to the nest with his throat or crop distended with tiny weed seeds, which he feeds to his mate by regurgitation. Skutch described the food as a "white, viscid mass," which suggests that something may have been added to the seeds, over and above partial digestion. One wonders whether there may be some fatty additive here along the lines of pigeon "milk." Similar masses of seeds are fed to the young, also by regurgitation.

The song of the goldfinch is as lilting, light, and bouncy as the bird's flight. It is especially sweet and high pitched. At any season of the year you may hear a gentle twittering while the birds are in flight. During the winter, when a few weed stalks remain above the frozen surface of the snow, the cheerful and vivacious companies of goldfinches are joined by relatives from farther north, such as pine siskins and common redpolls. In times of stress, the goldfinches will desert the open fields for birch and alder groves, and occasionally you will even find them in the heart of the forest. This is a matter of the availability of food, not of the temperature.

Length 4¹/₄ inches.   Male, Asheville, North Carolina, July 29.
Female, Athens, Georgia, May 26.

plate 104—the sketch

RUFOUS-SIDED TOWHEE
Pipilo erythrophthalmus

plate 104   # RUFOUS-SIDED TOWHEE *Pipilo erythrophthalmus*

IT would be difficult to mistake the towhee for any other bird; no species resembles it to any extent. This unusually good-looking finch customarily dwells on the ground, where it is often more difficult to see than its "splashy" pattern would indicate. Ornithologists regard the bird as a sort of "super-species" which occurs over almost all of the United States and in a strip across most of southern Canada, with the exception of western Ontario, Quebec, and the Maritimes.

Some fifteen different races, or subspecies, are recognized, and they reduce to essentially three major forms: the one illustrated, which has a black back and a red eye (the species used to be known as the red-eyed towhee); a southern form in which the iris of the eye is white; and the western bird, which is more or less heavily spotted with white on the back and wings. It has been decided, however, that these are all one species, and the rufous sides are common to all of them.

The female towhee is one of those females very handsome in their own right. In the spotted form, the head and back of the female are much darker than in the race illustrated; in fact, they are almost black.

The name of the bird is a valiant attempt to express its call, *to-whee*. Another common interpretation is *chewink*, which has also been used as a nick-name for the bird. The song is most frequently interpreted as *drink-your-teeeea*, consisting of two notes followed by a quavering trill. As Peterson so rightly observes, a verbalized description "conveys but a wretched idea of the voice of a bird." It does help, however, to give us some kind of reference for the next time we hear a particular sound. It is a kind of mental short-hand, really, and one which is very personal, because in every one of us hearing is just as individual as eyesight. Some basis for comparison usually helps, no matter how flimsy.

The towhee is a bird of dense brush, tangles, and thickets. One will rarely see one in a tree, except on those occasions when the male ascends to his singing perch. Even then, he makes frequent returns to ground level and the cover he requires. As they feed on the ground, the birds behave very like brown thrashers or fox sparrows. They work among the dead leaves with purpose and great vigour, often making a perceptible disturbance. A towhee will scratch with both feet at once, leaping into the air in order to do so, and the resulting turmoil on the forest floor sounds like the product of the efforts of a much larger animal. The purpose of the exercise is to get at insects in the humus during spring and summer, but when autumn comes the birds also eat a good deal of vegetable matter, including seeds and wild fruits of various kinds – as a proper sparrow's diet should be.

This is a tough species. It often winters a long distance north, even in southern Canada. Most of the population, however, appears to drift somewhat south for the coldest months, and they are absent then from the northernmost parts of their range. This is frequently a familiar bird at winter feeding stations, but only in those cases where there is sufficient adjacent cover to satisfy it. It is always careful to keep its distance.

Length 7¹/₄ inches.   Male, Atlanta, Georgia, March 30.
Female, Athens, Georgia, March 8.

plate 105—the sketch

SAVANNAH SPARROW

Passerculus sandwichensis

plate 105 # SAVANNAH SPARROW *Passerculus sandwichensis*

*A*NY small bird that lives, is fruitful, and multiplies from Alaska to Mexico and from Labrador to the West Indies, is hardy, adaptable, and (at least to some extent) opportunistic. All habitats seem apt for this abundant and attractive little sparrow. It survives in some of the most extreme conditions imaginable – barren seacoasts, arid deserts, chilly boglands, windswept sand dunes, as well as more congenial pastures and meadowlands. Its flexibility as a species in accommodating itself to this welter of varied environments is reflected in the fact that the American Ornithologists' Union recognized sixteen distinct subspecies in its most recent (1957) *Check-List.*

From the general, day-to-day point of view, subspecies are strictly for professional taxonomists working with museum specimens; they are of limited interest or value to field observers, simply because so many of them are not safely distinguishable in the field. But in this species the *extremes* are obvious, both in size and in colour. Usually the birds in the coldest parts of the range are the largest. Coloration can vary with habitat: paler birds on dunes and in deserts, darker birds in the forested regions. But these generalizations are elastic, and it takes a bird in the hand and an expert eye to distinguish the sundry forms. The bird illustrated is the typical nesting Savannah sparrow of the Canadian Maritime provinces.

Small sparrows are frustrating, to put it mildly, for the inexperienced bird watcher. Once one becomes familiar with some of the "basic" ones, however, one can gradually fill in the rest by the process of elimination. This species is exceptionally common in the right short-grass habitat. It is superficially like a song sparrow, in the sense that it is heavily streaked, and the streaks on the breast may converge to form a central spot in much the way they do on the song sparrow. However, the Savannah's crown has a pale central line, its tail is much shorter and has a notch at the end, and its legs are pink or flesh-coloured. It is perceptibly smaller than a song sparrow. Notice a yellowish line over the eye; in the spring a more pronounced yellow mark will develop *in front* of the eye.

A Savannah sparrow is extremely active on the ground. Usually it will hop about, but if one frightens it, it will take off mouselike through the grass at a dead run. The male commonly climbs up a grass stalk to sing. The song is thin, and buzzy, though soft. (Other "buzzing" sparrows are harsher, and sound more like insects.) Of the many and varied published descriptions of the song, I like Godfrey's – "A lisping *tsip, tsip, tsip, tsip, tse-wheeeeeeeeee-you* (the *wheeeeee* is trilled, the final *you* abrupt and much lower)." The Savannah's call note is an almost inaudible, sibilant *tseep*.

The name "Savannah" would seem to be extremely appropriate for this bird – wherever it may be in a geographic sense, it always seems to gravitate toward flat, open, grassy places. But in fact that is not the reason for the bird's name. It was named for Savannah, Georgia, by Wilson. The irony is that the bird does not in fact nest much south of New England, although it winters in considerable numbers right down the coast to Florida and beyond.

The migratory movements of the birds are exact. In South Carolina there has been a number of cases of banded birds returning to precisely the same place in successive winters. During that season, the many races are freely intermingled, but they seem to sort themselves out again for the spring journey northward.

Length 4³/₄ inches.   Female, Alligator Point, Florida.

plate 106—the sketch

VESPER SPARROW

Pooecetes gramineus

plate 106 # VESPER SPARROW *Pooecetes gramineus*

Tʜᴇ beginner will soon come to realize that sparrows are by no means as dull as he might have expected. None is more attractive than the vesper sparrow. It is immediately identifiable by the white outer feathers of its notched tail which are especially conspicuous when the bird flies. At closer range one will be able to see a slight eye-ring, a cheek patch, and a reddish "shoulder" patch, but the combination of typically sparrow-streaked upperparts and white tail flashes will confirm the identification.

The bird is a good singer. It does not limit itself to vespers, but is in fine voice all day long. Since it is willing to sing late in the day, sometimes after dark, we may perhaps hear it more clearly in the evening, after the competing and more abundant blackbirds, meadowlarks, and others have fallen silent. The song is pretty and characteristic; it "begins with two similar clear unhurried whistles, followed by higher ones and then by a descending jumble of twitters and trills" (Godfrey). The latter part of the song can be confused with that of the song sparrow, but the opening whistled notes are characteristic, and the combination of the two is diagnostic.

Although it frequents low places, the vesper sparrow likes them dry. Well-drained pastures are to its liking – places with short grass for cover, such as roadsides and burnt-over forest clearings. Unlike many songbirds, it may actually scratch a shallow depression in the ground before constructing its cup-shaped nest. As late spring and early summer grasses sprout and grow, a nest which may have been precariously visible a few weeks before can be completely obscured. Although its nest is at ground level, and the birds customarily forage there, the male chooses whatever eminence may be available from which to sing – a weed stalk, small bush, apple tree, fencepost, or telephone line.

Since vesper sparrows prefer the ground to be dry – even arid – it follows that, like so many other birds of such places, they often enjoy "dust-bathing." Obviously this dusting is not a matter of true bathing; it cannot accomplish the same result. Possibly it helps to get rid of small body parasites in some way analogous to the presumed purpose of "anting" (see orchard oriole, *plate 95*), but neither of these activities is properly understood. It is interesting, however, that there seem to be no reports of bird species which both dust *and* ant their feathers, so it may be reasonably safe to assume that the two activities have parallel functions in personal maintenance.

Sutton reported in Bent's *Life Histories* that the vesper sparrow does not seem to require a reliable water supply either for bathing or drinking. Many arid-country creatures are able to obtain sufficient moisture from dew and from the food they eat. As one might expect for such a sparrow, the vesper's diet consists largely of weed seeds, although it does also take a substantial number of insects. A certain amount of moisture is, of course, available in both.

The vesper sparrow breeds over most of the southern half of Canada (except western British Columbia) and the northern half of the United States. It winters in the southern states and Mexico. Although it is rarely out of earshot in the summer, the bird is by no means as common as, say, the song sparrow.

It seems to be comparatively quite demanding in terms of breeding territory. Berger has made this very interesting remark: "It seems likely that the number of pairs inhabiting extensive cultivated tracts planted to hay, wheat, or corn is limited by the number of available song perches rather than by actual territorial conflict." A provocative thought; territory involves much more than sheer acreage.

Length 5¹/₂ inches. Female, May 18.

plate 107 — the sketch

SLATE-COLORED JUNCO

Junco hyemalis

plate 107 # SLATE-COLORED JUNCO *Junco hyemalis*

JUNCOS are small sparrows, immediately recognizable by their even-coloured, unstreaked bodies and their conspicuous white outer tail feathers. There is at least one kind of junco in almost every place in North America south of the tundra. This species is by far the most numerous and widespread; it breeds south of the treeline in every Canadian province, and in those parts of the northeastern United States where there is a typically northern evergreen forest. Slate-colored juncos winter almost everywhere except southern Florida and the most arid parts of the southwest.

In the winter months most people are familiar with the juncos. Juncos roam snowy fields, hedgerows, backyards, and vacant lots in their search for weed seeds and the other simple fare of the season in small parties of a dozen or two. In their wanderings they mingle frequently with little bands of tree sparrows.

No matter what the season, juncos keep up an almost constant "talking" as they move about – a series of short, sharp *chip* notes as though to keep the individual members of a group in touch with each other at all times. This may also be a role of the white tail flashes, which very probably (as species identification markers) help birds of a feather to flock together. When one sees a small winter party of juncos, one may notice that they seem to move more purposefully and swiftly than most other birds, almost as though they had a definite goal in mind, as opposed to sheer nomadism.

The song of the slate-colored junco is a simple pleasing trill on one pitch, more musical than the drier trill of the chipping sparrow. Once I had the delightful experience of hearing a junco singing its "whisper song," a beautiful and lengthy *sotto voce* warble which was almost inaudible – completely unlike its regular song. I cannot help feeling that since the bird was a migrant and since the song under the circumstances could meet no mating or territorial need, that individual may simply have been enjoying the sound of his own voice. But that would be most difficult to prove.

We have five juncos in North America, and in areas where species overlap, several of them hybridize. In the East we have only the one breeding species, the slate-colored, but in winter we very occasionally have western visitors in the form of Oregon juncos. These birds are quite readily identified; they have a black head and hood in sharp contrast with a brown back and sides. However, intermediate birds do occasionally occur and it is safest not to call them Oregon juncos. The two interbreed in the Canadian Rockies.

The slate-colored junco was the subject of some pioneer studies by William Rowan of Edmonton, Alberta, who was interested in photoperiodicity and the way in which bird physiology and behaviour may be governed by seasonal changes in the length of day. Rowan exposed captive juncos to artificially lengthened days over a period of time, adjusting the electric lights in their cages so that the birds "thought" spring must be coming. When they were examined in midwinter, it was discovered that the sexual organs of birds so treated had become enlarged to spring breeding condition – in some of them, even to a greater size than "normal" birds were known to achieve in spring.

Length 5¹/₄ inches.   Male, Asheville, North Carolina, March 28.

plate 108—the sketch

CHIPPING SPARROW
Spizella passerina

plate 108 # CHIPPING SPARROW *Spizella passerina*

ITH the Savannah sparrow the chipping sparrow shares the distinction of being the smallest common sparrow in our area. In farmyards, village squares, and gardens any very tiny sparrow is almost certainly a chipping sparrow, with its (summer) red cap, white eye-line, and plain gray breast. Audubon claimed 130 years ago that it was one of the most common birds in the United States, and, keeping in mind the degree of agricultural development at that time, we have little reason to doubt his statement.

This sparrow shows a special liking for country plots, gardens, orchards, and even residential areas. It is particularly happy with open lawns sheltered by large shade trees. One could speculate that the relatively quiet towns and villages of Audubon's period, and the general pastoral nature of the land then settled, must have been ideal for this bird. Modern cities are not so attractive. Judging by the bird's willingness to live in proximity with man, one might guess that it may not have been so common a hundred years *before* Audubon, when so much of the land was still uncleared.

Of course, in the good old days, there were the horses. All the old bird books, without exception, emphasize the chipping sparrow's almost invariable use of horsehair with which to line its nest. In my boyhood that was one way of being sure of the identity of the nest without even seeing the bird or its eggs. With the decline of the horse population, however, things have changed, and the birds have to use substitutes. They will use any kind of animal hair when they can get it. In a remote part of Minnesota, where there were no horses, William DeMott Stull took with him some horsehair with which to bait chipping sparrows into his banding traps. He reports, in Bent's *Life Histories*, "It worked very well. At nest lining time the females readily entered traps containing a few strands of horse hair."

One wonders why this attraction to hair arose in these sparrows, birds which were unfamiliar with horses. Why has it persisted? Small songbirds are not long-lived creatures, and from his description of the area it is reasonable to assume that Stull's birds had had little if any previous experience with horse hair. The birds may well have had no more than one (if that) breeding season in their lives, yet they quickly used the ancestrally-favoured material when it became available.

Birds have some fascinating built-in predilections. I remember one of the Darwin's finches in the Galapagos, a *Geospiza scandens* (they have no English names) which availed itself of a beakful of Roger Tory Peterson's silver locks as he was being barbered by the Royal Ontario Museum's T. M. Shortt. Showing no fear, the bird hopped over and upon our feet to gather nesting material with which we were certain it had had no prior experience!

In early summer, one of the finer sounds is the loud trill of the chipping sparrow, uttered from some high vantage point. It consists of a series of dry *chips* uttered in such rapid succession that the individual notes melt together and form a continuous buzz. The voice of the pine warbler, which is sometimes confused with that of this bird, is very similar but slightly more musical. It is also ever so slightly slower, so that (to my ear) the individual notes are still distinguishable, albeit barely.

When feeding their young, chipping sparrows concentrate on insect food, but for the balance of the year their diet consists almost entirely of seeds, chiefly those of weeds of no economic significance. They winter in the southern states and beyond.

Length 4³/₄ inches.   Male, Clear Lake, Michigan, June 12.

plate 109—the sketch

FIELD SPARROW

Spizella pusilla

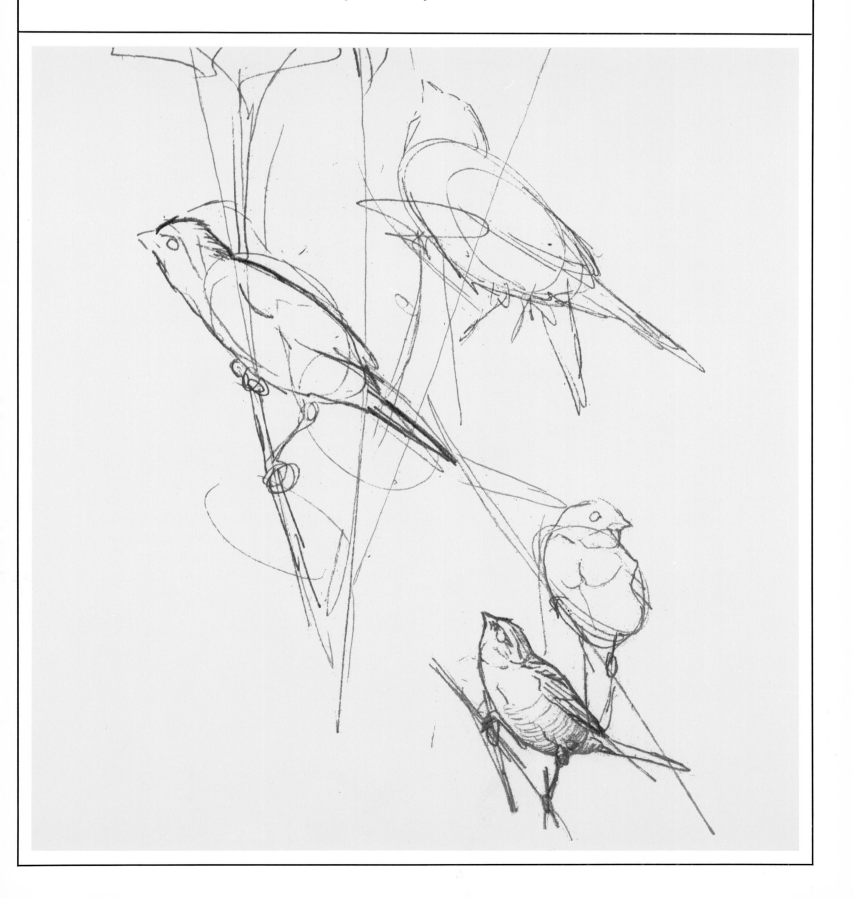

plate 109 # FIELD SPARROW *Spizella pusilla*

THE only sparrow with which this one can be confused in summertime is the chipping sparrow, which has a conspicuous black and white eye line and a dark bill. In winter, when our area entertains great flocks of tree sparrows from the subarctic, field sparrows are largely gone. The tree sparrow is bigger, brighter, and has a large black spot in the middle of its breast. The best clues to the field sparrow are its pinkish bill and legs, and its pale eye ring. Peterson, always uncannily apt (but, in this instance, somewhat ungracious) says of the field sparrow that it has a "blank" expression.

While it is not noted for its appearance, the field sparrow richly merits praise as a singer. Its distinctive song consists of a series of plaintive and high-pitched sweet whistles which begin slowly, then gradually accelerate into a trill, which at its conclusion may ascend or descend the scale, or remain steady. It is not a strong or powerful song, and one has to listen for it, but it is one of the more pleasant and appealing sounds of spring.

Males sing almost constantly while they are establishing territories and awaiting the arrival of the females, but then the song tapers off quite dramatically, and you will hear little further from them until the young are fledged and the birds are getting ready for a second (and perhaps third) brood.

Field sparrows are somewhat more stand-offish than some of their close relatives. They do not usually make use of human settlements and buildings; for the most part they eschew our company. But they are quite common, for all of that, and in suitably brushy fields and over-grown pastures they are often present in surprising numbers. The nest is usually on the ground, although small shrubs may be used later in the year. The most common enemy of field sparrows

seems to be the ever-present cowbird, but there seems to be no lessening of field sparrows on the cowbird's account. All ground nesters are of course subject to attack by the usual number of small predators – dogs, cats, squirrels, snakes, and all the rest.

Lawrence Walkinshaw, who has studied field sparrows in great depth, and who contributed the chapter on this species to Bent's *Life Histories*, has noted that not even the vigorous territorial singing of the males prevents occasional border incidents. One of the functions of song, of course, is to help define territorial boundaries. Field sparrows are also said to have a "specially patterned flight to intimidate territorial competitors." Walkinshaw noticed that the males "each came back to the identical spot he had defended the previous year." Now, the life of a small songbird is usually short, but Walkinshaw did have one male over six seasons. This individual had a different mate each of those years, but he remained constant to the mate of the year for two or three broods each summer. There are records of some female promiscuity: Walkinshaw observed one female which copulated with her mate and with two neighbouring males in swift succession.

Field sparrows nest over the greater part of the eastern United States, except the extreme south, and their normal range in Canada extends only into the southernmost parts of Ontario and Quebec. In winter they withdraw to the southern states, but one will see occasional individuals in the North at that season, usually mingling with tree sparrows. In the non-breeding season the birds are somewhat warmer in colour than they are at nesting time. The individual opposite, a late November bird in his wintering quarters in Florida, would have been slightly grayer in colour come spring.

Length 5 inches.   Male, Pensacola, Florida, November 24.

plate 110—the sketch

WHITE-THROATED SPARROW

Zonotrichia albicollis

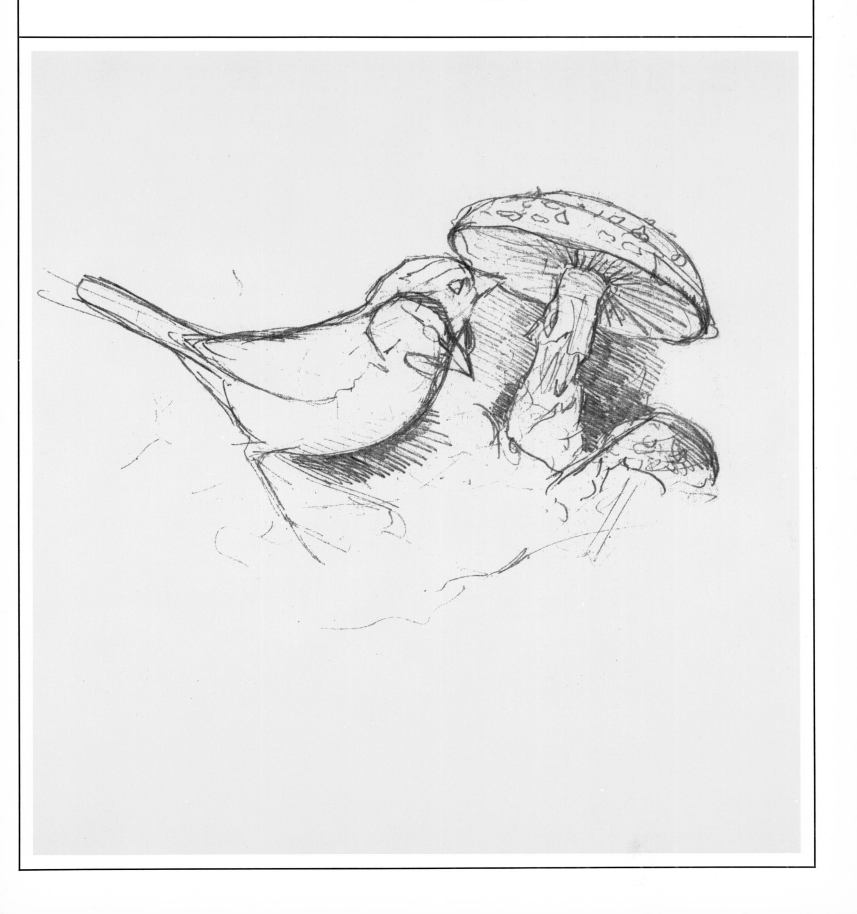

plate 110 # WHITE-THROATED SPARROW *Zonotrichia albicollis*

AFTER an apparently endless winter, the white-throat's song is an unfailing boost to morale. I feel certain that many more people are familiar with its song than know the bird's appearance. The clear, sweet but quavering notes are heard everywhere during spring migration – in the country, in city parks and gardens, and of course on the bird's nesting grounds in wooded areas mostly east of the mountains, from the Yukon to Newfoundland and Labrador, south to the Great Lakes and New England.

Surely I cannot be the only watcher of birds who spent almost an entire lifetime wondering, from time to time, why one sees brown-headed, apparently young white-throats in spring migration. They were not females, because the sexes are similar. But very few small songbirds come north to their breeding grounds in immature dress, and it was assumed until quite recently that fully adult garb was the one pictured here, complete with black and white stripes on the bird's crown.

Now, this question is resolved. Since 1958, James K. Lowther and J. Bruce Falls have been studying the white-throat on its breeding grounds, and in 1961 Lowther dropped the bombshell that the spring birds with brown-and-tan-striped heads were in fact adults, just as those with black-and-white heads are. The white-throat comes in two colour types, and the two interbreed. This was a new and fascinating development in our understanding of a bird which is so common that most of us simply took it for granted.

According to Lowther and Falls, who worked with white-throats for several years in Ontario's Algonquin Provincial Park, four-fifths of the nests they examined had incorporated some kind of "structural canopy" such as that afforded by clumps of dead ferns and grasses. They report, in Bent's *Life Histories*, that only the female builds the nest, which is usually "on the ground at the edge of a clearing." There are occasional records of white-throats nesting above ground level.

An interesting observation sheds light on the way in which somewhat similar birds "share" the available landscape in their choices of nesting sites. The authors report that the white-throats choose conditions "intermediate between the open areas in which song sparrows nest and the dense woodland in which juncos nest." Thus, three very closely related species can live at very close quarters, and without competition can make the optimum use of the opportunities offered by their environment.

No characteristic of the white-throat is so memorable as its song. A series of whistled notes, which usually change in pitch in the course of the song, it takes a characteristic pattern, of which the best known is the tendency to be grouped in "triplets" interspersed with steady notes. The traditional interpretation of the song has been *Poor Sam Peabody, Peabody, Peabody,* or, depending upon where you may be listening to it, *Oh sweet Canada, Canada, Canada.* At one period, the word *Kennedy* was elicited at the expense of *Canada.* Falls remarks that the more usual form, as described by Borror and Gunn, comes out thus: *Poor Peabody, Sam, Peabody, Peabody, Peabody.* Whatever the form, however, the plaintive quality of the white-throat's whistle is almost instantly recognizable most of the time, and the typical three-syllable *Peabody* is unmistakable.

As this is being written (mid-October) a white-throat is bathing with spirit and vigour in a small puddle formed in a depression in some fallen leaves, within two feet of my window. It has a head with brown and tan stripes. Before 1961 I would not have given it a second look. Now, however, I shall never know whether it is in fact an adult of the brown-and-tan form or a young bird. . .

Length 5³/₄ inches. Male, Herndon, Virginia, April 24.

plate 111—the sketch

SWAMP SPARROW

Melospiza georgiana

plate 111 SWAMP SPARROW *Melospiza georgiana*

THE large and world-wide family of seed-eating finches is represented on all continents except Antarctica where, at the moment, there are no seeds to eat. There are nearly seven hundred species of these birds, and almost half of them are thought to have originated in the New World. Our birds vary tremendously in appearance, from the showy, brilliant cardinal and indigo bunting to the unobtrusive brown and streaked sparrows.

What seed-eating finches have in common, among other things, is the stout, conical bill and heavy jaw muscles with which they crack the hard shells of the seeds they live on for the greater part of the year. The size of the bill can range from the massive and heavy equipment of the evening grosbeak to the slender, almost delicate beak of the swamp sparrow and some of its relatives. The swamp sparrow happens to be more committed to a diet of insects than some of the other *Melospiza* sparrows, and this is evidenced in its lighter bill and, anatomists tell us, its smaller skull.

Of course, any species is simply a convenient and arbitrary expression of a moment in time: tomorrow's swamp sparrow may not look like today's – or yesterday's. In the tropics, where one sees a wider variety of small birds of this kind, it is often difficult to decide whether the bird one is looking at is finch, tanager, or blackbird. Intermediate forms abound, and perhaps the swamp sparrow is on its way to becoming a new kind of little marsh "blackbird," and not a finch at all.

This is a shy, furtive, and (except when it is singing) unobtrusive bird of marshes, swamps, and wherever there is grassy vegetation and shallow water. It likes large cat-tail marshes, but nests also in rank growth at the edges of streams, ponds, and bays. It has often been observed to feed by actually wading in the water. Such places abound with insects in season, and, like its neighbours the yellowthroats and the long-billed marsh wrens, the swamp sparrow makes a relatively easy living.

The bird is not much to look at – rather a dark sparrow, with reddish crown and wings. At closer range one will notice the pale throat and gray breast. The swamp sparrow is most readily identified by its voice, and in the breeding season it is notably vociferous. The song is a series of *chips* strung together so quickly as to become a trill. It is much louder than that of the chipping sparrow, noticeably slower, and somewhat more musical. The call note is an emphatic metallic *chink*. Like the marsh wren, the swamp sparrow will readily sing at night.

A swamp sparrow's nest may be on the ground, in grass tussocks, or in the tangled lower stalks of cat-tails, or in low bushes. Wherever they are placed, the nests are critically vulnerable to rapidly changing water levels, and many a brood has been wiped out by sudden flooding. As Wetherbee puts it, in Bent's *Life Histories*, "Each year the birds take two or three of these 20-day gambles, that the water will not rise until their young are fledged." The period referred to is about twelve days for the incubation of the eggs, and another nine or so for the young to leave the nest. It all happens in quite a hurry. But then small birds do not have much time – their lives are short.

Length 5 inches. New Jersey, April 23.

plate 112—the sketch

SONG SPARROW

Melospiza melodia

plate 112   SONG SPARROW *Melospiza melodia*

NYONE attempting to learn the sparrows should begin by acquainting himself thoroughly with the song sparrow, so abundant almost everywhere as to be *the* yardstick for the identification of some of the less common species. The song sparrow is brown, and it is streaked, as are so many sparrows. It has especially heavy markings on the back and sides, and the streaks on the breast converge to a central spot. The tail is rather long (several somewhat similar species have much shorter tails). The bird has a habit of working it up and down as it flies. This habit is especially noticeable when the song sparrow drops down into a shrub or other cover – the tail gives a final derisive flick as the bird disappears. Notice the head and face markings. Once one has learned this sparrow thoroughly, one will have much less difficulty with the others.

Song sparrows are found in summer over a vast portion of the continent – from Alaska and Newfoundland to Mexico and the Carolinas. But they are not all the same song sparrows. To make the best possible use of the varying kinds of habitat in that enormous area, the song sparrow has demonstrated the height of adaptability as a species. Thirty-one separate subspecies were recognized in the most recent A.O.U. *Check-List*, which makes the song sparrow the most variable bird we have.

This wide splitting-up of a species is evolution in action. Every race, should it become sufficiently isolated from the others, is potentially a new species. Looking at a random collection of the many races on a museum table – some large, some small, some dusky, some pale – one will wonder immediately how long it will take until there are more than one song sparrow species. It is rather like looking at the wide assortment of Galapagos

finches today. Birds descended from a common ancestor begin to look and act different from each other as they invade different kinds of habitat and take up different styles of living.

Except for the swamp sparrow, we have few finches – or any other songbirds, for that matter – which show such an affinity for water. Song sparrows are found almost wherever there is fresh water, from open ponds to soggy ground, with enough brush and dense cover to suit their foraging and nesting purposes.

Nests are placed either right at the level of the ground or at a modest height above it. Depending upon the length of summer (and thus the latitude), the weather, and other circumstances, song sparrows may raise two, three, or even four broods of young in the course of a season. When conditions are good, breeding territories are quite small, and song sparrows will nest at unusually close quarters with their own species. Their nests are heavily parasitized by cowbirds and, like others at such low levels, the nests are vulnerable to predators. But the clutches run from three to six eggs, and as in most small birds there is a mortality of about eighty per cent.

The song sparrow sings throughout spring and summer, and is even heard sometimes in the dead of winter. It is difficult to generalize about the song. Typically, in our region, it "begins with two or three loud notes which sound like *sweet, sweet, sweet*, followed by a trill, then several short notes that run down to the end of the song" (Godfrey). I was brought up on the dreadful verbalization "*Hip, hip, hurray, boys, spring is here!*" The call note is almost impossible to describe; it is a distinctive, short metallic chirp. The best thing to do is to isolate a song sparrow, memorize its call note, and proceed from there.

Length 5¹/₂ inches.   Male, Stafford, Virginia, December 6.

Bibliography and Index

Bibliography

*The birdwatcher is blessed with an extremely wide range of reading —
from books especially for the beginner to the vast advanced literature
of ornithology. The selection of titles presented here does not pretend
to be more than a sample of the sources available; it is offered merely as
an introduction to the subject, and includes both elementary and more
advanced references.*

Identification

PETERSON, ROGER TORY, *A Field Guide to the Birds*. Boston: Houghton
Mifflin, 1947.

POUGH, RICHARD H., *Audubon Land Bird Guide*. Garden City: Doubleday, 1946. *Audubon Water Bird Guide*. Garden City: Doubleday, 1951.

ROBBINS, CHANDLER S., BRUNN, BERTEL, *and* ZIM, HERBERT S., *illustrated by*
ARTHUR SINGER, *Birds of North America*. New York: Golden Press, 1966.

*These books are visual aids to bird identification. In many cases, how-
ever, the song or call note of a bird may serve as corroboration of a
sighting, and occasionally may be even more important than the appearance of a bird. A number of long-play bird recordings of excellent
quality has appeared in recent years, and the number is growing. Some
are collections of birds of geographic regions; others contain families of
birds. For details, the reader is referred to the Federation of Ontario
Naturalists, Don Mills, Ontario, Canada.*

General and Reference

AMERICAN ORNITHOLOGISTS' UNION, *Check-list of North American Birds*
(5th edition). Baltimore: A.O.U., 1957.

AUSTIN, OLIVER L. JR., *and* SINGER, ARTHUR, *Birds of the World*. New York:
Golden Press, 1961.

BENT, ARTHUR C., *Life Histories of North American Birds* (21 vols.).
Washington: United States National Museum, 1919-1968.

BERGER, ANDREW J., *Bird Study*. New York: J. Wiley and Sons, 1961.

CRUICKSHANK, ALLAN *and* HELEN, *1001 Questions Answered About Birds*.
New York: Dodd, Mead, 1958.

DARLING, LOIS *and* LOUIS, *Bird*. Boston: Houghton Mifflin, 1962.

DORST, JEAN, *The Migrations of Birds*. Boston: Houghton Mifflin, 1963.

FISHER, JAMES, *and* PETERSON, ROGER TORY, *The World of Birds*. Garden
City: Doubleday, 1963.

FORBUSH, E. H., *and* MAY, JOHN B., *A Natural History of the Birds of
Eastern and Central North America*. Boston: Houghton Mifflin, 1939.

HALL, HENRY MARION, *edited by* ROLAND C. CLEMENT, *A Gathering of Shore
Birds*. New York: Devin Adair, 1960.

HICKEY, J. J., *A Guide to Bird Watching*. New York: Oxford University
Press, 1943.

KORTRIGHT, F. H., *Ducks, Geese and Swans of North America*. Washington: American Wildlife Institute, 1942.

LINCOLN, FREDERICK C., *Migration of Birds*. Washington: United States
Department of the Interior, Fish and Wildlife Service Circular 16, 1950.

PALMER, RALPH S. (ed.), *Handbook of North American Birds* (Vol. 1). New Haven: Yale University Press, 1962.

PETERSON, ROGER TORY (ed.), *The Bird Watcher's Anthology*. New York: Harcourt, Brace, 1957. *Birds Over America*. New York: Dodd, Mead, 1964.

PETERSON, ROGER TORY, *The Bird Watcher's Anthology* (ed.), New York: Time Inc., 1963.

PETTINGILL, OLIN SEWALL JR., *A Guide to Bird Finding (East)*. New York: Oxford University Press, 1951. (ed.), *The Bird Watcher's America*. New York: McGraw-Hill, 1965.

THOMSON, A. LANDSBOROUGH (ed.), *A New Dictionary of Birds*. London: Nelson, 1964.

VAN TYNE, JOSSELYN, *and* BERGER, ANDREW J., *Fundamentals of Ornithology*. New York: J. Wiley and Sons, 1959.

WELTY, JOEL CARL, *The Life of Birds*. New York: Alfred A. Knopf, 1963.

Canadian

GODFREY, W. EARL, *The Birds of Canada*. Ottawa: National Museum of Canada Bulletin No. 203, 1966.

LIVINGSTON, JOHN A., *illustrated by* J. FENWICK LANSDOWNE, *Birds of the Northern Forest*. Toronto: McClelland and Stewart; Boston: Houghton Mifflin, 1966.

MUNRO, J. A., *and* COWAN, IAN MCTAGGART, *A Review of the Bird Fauna of British Columbia*. Victoria: B.C. Provincial Museum, Special Publication No. 2, 1947.

PETERS, H. S. *and* BURLEIGH, T. D., *The Birds of Newfoundland*. St. John's: Newfoundland Department of Natural Resources, 1951.

SALT, W. RAY, *and* WILK, A. L., *The Birds of Alberta*. Edmonton: Alberta Department of Economic Affairs, 1958.

SNYDER, L. L., *Ontario Birds*. Toronto: Clarke, Irwin, 1950.

SQUIRES, W. AUSTIN, *The Birds of New Brunswick*. Saint John: The New Brunswick Museum (Monographic Series No. 4), 1952.

TAVERNER, P. A., *Birds of Canada*. Ottawa: Canadian Department of Mines Bulletin No. 72, 1934.

TUFTS, ROBIE W., *The Birds of Nova Scotia*. Halifax: Nova Scotia Museum, 1961.

Periodicals

There are many publications produced regularly by local, provincial and other bird clubs and organizations. The following brief selection is considered fundamental for the birdwatcher in this region:

AMERICAN ORNITHOLOGISTS' UNION, *The Auk*.

CANADIAN AUDUBON SOCIETY, *Canadian Audubon*.

FEDERATION OF ONTARIO NATURALISTS, *The Ontario Naturalist*.

NATIONAL AUDUBON SOCIETY, *Audubon*.

SASKATCHEWAN NATURAL HISTORY SOCIETY, *The Blue Jay*.

WILSON ORNITHOLOGICAL SOCIETY, *The Wilson Bulletin*.

Index

Items in brown are to be found in volume II.

On the Making of this Book

The type chosen is Palatino,
a design created by Hermann Zapf for
Stempel Linotype, Frankfurt, and first issued in 1950.
It is a Roman face with broad letters and strong, inclined serifs
resembling the Venetian. Named after the sixteenth-century Italian
writing master Palatino, this type is highly legible and
has retained the aesthetic sculptural
form of the Venetian letter.

Type was set in Canada by Howarth & Smith Monotype, Limited, Toronto

The book was printed and bound in Verona by
Arnoldo Mondadori, Officine Grafiche. The
paintings were reproduced by five-colour lithography on "NEP Three Star" paper. The intro-
ductory pages and endmatter were printed by
lithography on "Tenax Ventura" paper.

The drawings on pages preceding the plates were reproduced
from J. Fenwick Lansdowne's preliminary sketches.